NEW DIRECTIONS FOR EVALUATION
A Publication of the American Evaluation Association

Gary T. Henry, *Georgia State University*
EDITOR-IN-CHIEF

Jennifer C. Greene, *Cornell University*
EDITOR-IN-CHIEF

Progress and Future Directions in Evaluation: Perspectives on Theory, Practice, and Methods

Debra J. Rog
Vanderbilt University

Deborah Fournier
Boston University

EDITORS

Number 76, Winter 1997

JOSSEY-BASS PUBLISHERS
San Francisco

PROGRESS AND FUTURE DIRECTIONS IN EVALUATION: PERSPECTIVES ON THE-
ORY, PRACTICE, AND METHODS
Debra J. Rog, Deborah Fournier (eds.)
New Directions for Evaluation, no. 76
Jennifer C. Greene, Gary T. Henry, Editors-in-Chief

Microfilm copies of issues and articles are available in 16mm and 35mm,
as well as microfiche in 105mm, through University Microfilms Inc., 300
North Zeeb Road, Ann Arbor, Michigan 48106-1346.

New Directions for Evaluation is indexed in Contents Pages in Education,
Higher Education Abstracts, and Sociological Abstracts.

ISSN 0164-7989   ISBN 0-7879-3955-2

NEW DIRECTIONS FOR EVALUATION is part of The Jossey-Bass Education
Series and is published quarterly by Jossey-Bass Inc., Publishers, 350
Sansome Street, San Francisco, California 94104-1342.

SUBSCRIPTIONS cost $63.00 for individuals and $105.00 for institutions,
agencies, and libraries. Prices subject to change.

EDITORIAL CORRESPONDENCE should be addressed to the Editors-in-Chief,
Jennifer C. Greene, Department of Policy Analysis and Management, MVR
Hall, Cornell University, Ithaca, NY 14853-4401, or Gary T. Henry,
School of Policy Studies, Georgia State University, P.O. Box 4039, Atlanta,
GA 30302-4039.

Jossey-Bass Web address: http://www.josseybass.com

Manufactured in the United States of America using Lyons Falls D Anthology
paper, which is a special blend of non-tree fibers and totally chlorine-free
wood pulp.

EDITORIAL POLICY AND PROCEDURES

New Directions for Evaluation, a quarterly sourcebook, is an official publication of the American Evaluation Association. The journal publishes empirical, methodological, and theoretical works on all aspects of evaluation. A reflective approach to evaluation is an essential strand to be woven through every volume. The editors encourage volumes that have one of three foci: (1) craft volumes that present approaches, methods, or techniques that can be applied in evaluation practice, such as the use of templates, case studies, or survey research; (2) professional issue volumes that present issues of import for the field of evaluation, such as utilization of evaluation or locus of evaluation capacity; (3) societal issue volumes that draw out the implications of intellectual, social, or cultural developments for the field of evaluation, such as the women's movement, communitarianism, or multiculturalism. A wide range of substantive domains is appropriate for *New Directions for Evaluation;* however, the domains must be of interest to a large audience within the field of evaluation. We encourage a diversity of perspectives and experiences within each volume, as well as creative bridges between evaluation and other sectors of our collective lives.

The editors do not consider or publish unsolicited single manuscripts. Each issue of the journal is devoted to a single topic, with contributions solicited, organized, reviewed, and edited by a guest editor. Issues may take any of several forms, such as a series of related chapters, a debate, or a long article followed by brief critical commentaries. In all cases, the proposals must follow a specific format, which can be obtained from the editor-in-chief. These proposals are sent to members of the editorial board and to relevant substantive experts for peer review. The process may result in acceptance, a recommendation to revise and resubmit, or rejection. However, the editors are committed to working constructively with potential guest editors to help them develop acceptable proposals.

Jennifer C. Greene, Editor-in-Chief
Department of Policy Analysis and Management
MVR Hall
Cornell University
Ithaca, NY 14853-4401
e-mail: jcg8@cornell.edu

Gary T. Henry, Editor-in-Chief
School of Policy Studies
Georgia State University
P.O. Box 4039
Atlanta, GA 30302-4039
e-mail: gthenry@gsu.edu

CONTENTS

EDITORS' NOTES

Last year, the American Evaluation Association celebrated its tenth anniversary. The annual conference, held in November 1996 and entitled *AEA: A Decade of Progress, Looking Back and Looking Forward,* provided an opportunity to review the history and status of the field of evaluation and chart future directions. As conference cochairs, we invited Plenary and Presidential Strand speakers who have contributed notable scholarship through the development and refinement of methodology, theory, and practice. In this volume, we solicited papers from some of these speakers to offer an array of perspectives on where the field has been and where it should be going.

By no means does this volume offer a comprehensive treatment of evaluation issues. There were many more conference papers that we would have liked to include in this collection, as well as many more we would have liked to commission. However, with contributions from this host of seasoned evaluators, this volume addresses some of the more significant developments in the field, highlights some critical concerns, and signals some new directions. In this introduction, we outline common themes, followed by a brief review of the chapters.

Developments in the Field

Increasing Emphasis on Theory. The concept of theory has taken a strong hold in evaluation. In Chapter Three, Carol H. Weiss traces theory-based evaluation as far back as the early 1970s but notes that it was in the late 1980s that program theory was a visible concept in evaluation. For example, during that time, three issues of this journal were devoted to the topic, along with numerous articles and several books. Theory of evaluation practice also emerged in the 1980s.

Several of the authors, all of whom have previously written about the use of program theory in evaluation, weave the concept through their chapters. Weiss's entire chapter is on the topic, providing a brief historical review of theory-based evaluation as well as perspectives on where we are and where we should be headed. Robert K. Yin, in Chapter Six, stresses the importance of logic models in advancing the practice of case study evaluations, and, in Chapter Seven, Joseph S. Wholey illustrates their continued importance in examining the theory underlying the Government Performance and Results Act (GPRA), a recently passed federal law requiring the use of planning and performance measurement to improve management and program effectiveness, policy decision making, and public confidence in government.

In Chapter One, Mark W. Lipsey extends the discussion of theory by making the case for evaluators to contribute to the theory of social interventions. Finally, Thomas A. Schwandt, in Chapter Two, shifts the discussion on theory to evaluation theory and one aspect of evaluation theory, namely, values. His discussion exposes limitations of our traditional social science stance and highlights different ways to construe practice and the associated consequences, providing directions for future dialogue in evaluation theory.

Use of Mixed Methods. The merits of mixed methods have been recognized in the last decade, replacing the often divisive arguments of one method's superiority over the other with a more constructive approach of their melding and joint use. The chapters in this volume are not preoccupied with philosophical differences in paradigms; rather, they are more concerned with working toward integrating methods to draw defensible conclusions. Several chapters suggest the merits of mixed methods. In Chapter Six, for example, Judith M. Gueron, in her review of welfare-to-work evaluations, highlights the importance of randomized experiments but also points out the contributions of qualitative studies.

Multiple Studies. A consistent theme in evaluation (as well as other social science areas) has been the value of conducting and synthesizing multiple studies. Robert K. Yin, in Chapter Seven, for example, describes the role that multiple-case studies can play in examining and testing rival theories and explanation. Gueron ascribes at least part of the impact evaluation has had in the area of welfare reform to the fact that multiple randomized experiments were conducted over the course of the last decade or more, developing a body of work that contributed a set of conclusions and directions for the field.

The need to synthesize our growing knowledge also has attained increasing attention. Lipsey discusses the need to integrate studies to develop social intervention theory, and Weiss describes the need to integrate ideas and concepts to improve our own practices. Lipsey and Peter H. Rossi (in Chapter Four) both touch on the importance of meta-analysis as a tool to integrate our findings from numerous studies.

Evaluation Impact. Since the 1970s, evaluators have struggled to make their practice useful to decision makers. The authors note a number of ways in which evaluation has an impact. Gueron, as noted, describes the impressive role that randomized studies have had in guiding past welfare changes; she notes that with the current welfare reforms, however, evaluators may not be able to continue this level of inquiry and should develop alternative methods for developing credible and convincing information. Wholey describes the impact that evaluators can have in the federal arena during this period of heightened focus on performance measurement, and Lipsey discusses the role that evaluators can have in the broader arena of social intervention.

Understanding the Underlying Mechanisms. Evaluation has historically been "outcome" oriented. As evaluators, we are often charged with finding the answer to the question "Did it work?" As Weiss and Lipsey both stress, however, an evaluation can provide a much greater and broader contribution if it is also designed to study the mediating mechanisms between process and outcome.

The Organization of This Volume

In Chapter One, Mark Lipsey, one of the two plenary speakers at the 1996 AEA conference, argues that, although we have conducted thousands of evaluations on social interventions, there has been little effort to cumulate that knowledge in a manner that can guide the architects of these interventions. He highlights two routes for cumulating this knowledge: building social intervention theory and meta-analysis. Social intervention theory characterizes the nature and effectiveness of categories of social programs and can be developed through a synthesis of past evaluations. This theory can help evaluators to take on new studies and program practitioners to plan and implement programs. In addition, meta-analysis, though commonly used to determine the average effects of similar outcome studies, could be used to reveal patterns in the findings within one or more intervention areas.

In Chapter Two, Tom Schwandt critically examines moral values and normative criteria in evaluation. Schwandt begins with an overview of the ways in which values have been discussed in evaluation and explains why developments have been slow to emerge. He then shifts to an overview of our social science legacy and describes several alternate frameworks from which to view and examine evaluation practice. For example, in one framework the aim of evaluation is to service social justice by emancipating marginalized groups; in an alternate framework, the purpose of evaluation is to foster dialogue to cultivate practical wisdom. Schwandt contends that evaluators are not solely social scientists with technical expertise in scientific methods but also make value claims about programs, policies, and interventions. In doing so, we shape a conception of social good. He provides a clarification of how values and ethics manifest themselves in everyday practice and leaves the reader thinking more critically about the ethical assumptions from which he or she operates when conducting evaluations.

In Chapter Three, Carol Weiss reviews the evolution of theory-based evaluation from the late 1960s to the present. At present, she argues, we are putting our ideas and approaches of program theory to the test. Weiss stresses the importance of elaborating theory so that we can better understand program implementation and the mediating mechanisms between process and outcomes. Like Lipsey, she believes that evaluation could contribute to the cumulation of theoretical knowledge on interventions if they can focus more on the pathways that lead to program effects and if they are conducted on central assumptions in multiple studies to provide for a meta-analysis of the studies across a range of conditions.

Peter H. Rossi, in Chapter Four, summarizes a decade of advances in quantitative methods. He begins with an overview of the advances that have facilitated evaluation work, such as developments in computing, data collection, access to datasets, and communication through computers. He then reviews advances in measurement, including statistical improvements in dealing with missing values and correcting for statistical inference measures, the development of the factorial survey method, and improvements in experimentation with question wording so we better understand how responses are affected by the way we construct questions. Lastly, Rossi highlights advances in statistical analyses, such as hierarchical linear modeling, selection bias modeling, meta-analysis, analysis of categorical data, and drawing inferences from multistate samples.

Robert Yin, in Chapter Five, provides a historical perspective of the case study in evaluation and discusses its progress in the past decade. Whereas the late 1970s and early 1980s saw increased documentation of the case study, in the last ten years there has been increased use of the case study and, in turn, refinement and elaboration of the method. As Yin discusses, case studies are now recognized as having specific tools (such as the case study protocol and logic models) and rigor. The case study has become a legitimate, formal research method in evaluation. Yin cautions that it is too soon, however, to determine whether the improvements in the case study craft itself have led to improvements in the case studies conducted.

The last two chapters focus on specific substantive areas of evaluation. In Chapter Six, Judith Gueron describes the role that rigorous evaluations of welfare-to-work programs have had in shaping social policy and program practice. This body of work tested different areas of welfare reform using randomized experiments, with the majority focused on state-level mandatory programs. Throughout the 1980s, the studies were credited with having a large effect on federal and state welfare policy and for reducing the uncertainty on the costs, impacts, and feasibility of this area of intervention. From these studies, Gueron draws out a number of lessons for evaluators that inform how we work with stakeholders, the types of methodological approaches we take, and the ways in which we try to disseminate the information and foster use. With the current and likely future changes in welfare, it is unclear whether this high level of rigor (especially the use of randomized experiments) and impact can continue. Gueron challenges evaluators to strive for developing research strategies in this new era that can provide for convincing and policy-responsive results.

In the final chapter, Joe Wholey describes the implications of the Government Performance and Results Act of 1993 (P.L. 103-62) for evaluator involvement. As Wholey notes, the implicit theory behind the Act is that planning and performance measurement will, in turn, improve program management, program effectiveness, policy decision making, and overall public confidence in government. Wholey describes a series of studies testing this theory that suggest it may be accurate. For evaluators, Wholey notes that the activities initiated by GPRA require the skills and experience that evaluators have to offer. Whether it is assisting agencies in the front-end implementation of the Act by identifying appropriate and measurable goals and appropriate measures or in collecting, analyzing, and interpreting performance information, evaluators can play a key role.

Summary

This volume's seven authors collectively offer a review of the last decade of evaluation and offer perspectives on its current status and future directions. Although several themes are noted, one cross-cutting theme emerges as a guiding beacon for the future. Evaluators, whether conducting a single study or a set of studies, are contributing to a broader enterprise. In doing so, we must be more cognizant of our responsibility to design and implement our studies with this broader contribution in mind.

Debra J. Rog
Deborah Fournier
Editors

DEBRA J. ROG is a research fellow at the Vanderbilt University Institute for Public Policy Studies, where she directs the Washington office of the Center for Mental Health Policy.

DEBORAH FOURNIER is an assistant professor at Boston University and the director of Educational Research and Evaluation at the Goldman School of Dental Medicine.

Combining evaluation studies and evaluation designs and studying program processes can lead to the building of better social intervention theories needed to guide effective program development and evaluation design.

What Can You Build with Thousands of Bricks? Musings on the Cumulation of Knowledge in Program Evaluation

Mark W. Lipsey

Once upon a time there was a tribe of brick makers who were extraordinary craftspersons. They made bricks to order for a wide range of important customers. They made qualitative bricks, quantitative bricks, and mixed method bricks; summative and formative bricks; decision-oriented and utilization-focused bricks; stakeholder and theory-driven bricks; fourth- and fifth-generation bricks; bricks that empowered and bricks that were responsive, and even an occasional goal-free brick. These bricks served many wonderful and useful purposes: they were used to support successful programs, hold open doors and windows of opportunity, buttress managerial decisions, quash failed efforts, add substance to political opinion, anchor outcomes, and generally fortify merit and worth against the evil forces of partisan attack, bureaucratic ineptness, and the null hypothesis. After these bricks were used so well and were no longer fresh, however, they often ended up on shelves gathering dust or stacked in dark corners of offices and libraries. Indeed, many quite elegant ones went to such places directly, perhaps being too hot to handle, delivered too late to be useful, or too heavy for the users to bear.

After some years the landscape was covered with bricks of many different sorts and sizes. A few brick makers began to ask if something interesting and useful could not be built with all these bricks. Some argued that what could be built with them might be as useful and important as the individual bricks themselves. Several went so far as to suggest that new bricks be crafted in such a way that they would be more useful for building something after they were used for their more immediate purposes. Needless to say, other brick makers thought these notions were a foolish waste of time and were not even what the craft of brick making was all about. Nonetheless, a few eccentric brick makers put aside their brick-making tools and began to collect used bricks and assemble them into different configurations to see what they might build from them. They soon learned to make interesting and useful constructions by stacking and arranging the thousands of bricks their colleagues had fashioned. And thus was born a new craft among the brick makers, the craft of building edifices from bricks or, as some liked to call it, meta–brick making.[1]

Program evaluation is much like brick making in this parable. Each evaluation is carefully crafted for a particular program, sponsor, situation, and need. And when this is well done, the results are useful for the program and its stakeholders, but it may have little consequence beyond that immediate context. But is the sum total of cumulative knowledge produced by the thousands of evaluations of social programs no more than a piecemeal collection of individual findings with localized application? Or can some larger structures be constructed with all these studies that will have value in their own right?

In this paper, I make the case for the value of efforts to synthesize at least parts of the recorded knowledge that the evaluation field and related areas have produced about the structure, performance, and effects of social programs. We have accumulated a great deal of knowledge about the methods and procedures with which such programs can be studied, but surprisingly little about the general nature of social intervention itself. I address this topic under two headings: *theory* and *meta-analysis*.

Theory

Many people have written about *program theory* in evaluation, referring to the assumptions about the change process through which programs bring about their intended outcomes. In the early formulation by Weiss (1972), the Chen and Rossi writings (1980, 1983; Chen, 1990), the papers in the two volumes of *New Directions for Program Evaluation* edited by Bickman (1987, 1990), and some of my own work (Lipsey and Pollard, 1989; Lipsey, 1993), for instance, explication of the theory, or *logic model*, inherent in a program has been advocated as a way to improve the design of the evaluation and as a framework for interpreting its results. In this form, program theory gives the evaluator guidance about the variables to investigate, the relationships expected among them, and their role in program success or failure.

However, such program theory, like most evaluation projects, tends to be ad hoc and piecemeal, crafted for a specific program application with no need to be generalizable beyond that situation. What I have in mind instead is broader intervention theory that characterizes the nature and effectiveness of whole categories of social programs and synthesizes information gleaned from numerous evaluation studies. Just as Boyle's law of gases or Darwinian evolutionary theory provides a small number of concepts and principles that account for a wide range of specific events and phenomena, there are likely to be general concepts and principles that account for a wide range of program situations. Or, put the other way, each social program is probably not so unique that it does not share any forms and processes with other programs. The objective of intervention theory is to describe those common forms and processes in ways that reveal which differences are important and which are not.

Consider some of the advantages of having well-developed social intervention theory. First, of course, refined images of the nature and effects of broad categories of social intervention would help us better ascertain the key aspects of the programs we evaluate and thus help us conduct better evaluations. While not neglecting the idiosyncracies of each program studied, we could draw on intervention theory to identify the general form of the program process being studied and, with that, be alerted to those issues most likely to be crucial for program success. Indeed, good evaluators do something like this now when they try to identify the underlying assumptions connecting program activities to the intended outcomes as an initial step in describing a program and planning an evaluation. What I am suggesting is that better codification of what we have learned from decades of experience about the general nature of those processes would greatly facilitate our efforts.

Second, more fully developed social intervention theory would be invaluable for program planning and implementation. Useful theory would provide guidance to planners and managers regarding the forms of intervention most likely to work for particular types of situations and those that have little prospect for success. Intervention theory is thus one of the links we need to close the loop between the evaluation of existing programs and the design of new or improved programs. Feedback from the cumulated knowledge gained through evaluating thousands of past and present programs should be available in efficient form to help successive generations of programs become progressively better.

What is remarkable is that so much program evaluation has been completed and reported since evaluation emerged as a distinct field of study about thirty years ago but so little effort has been invested in seeking general patterns in those findings. Perhaps we have been trained so well to recognize the unique aspects of each program and tailor our evaluations accordingly that we find it difficult to observe the substantial similarities among many programs and the problems they address. Or perhaps this applied field of evaluation simply offers its practitioners too little opportunity to reflect on these broader patterns amid the pressures of keeping up with the latest techniques, meeting report deadlines, and negotiating and planning the next evaluation. In any event, although there are research reviews of what has been found from evaluation in a specific program area—for example, drug prevention programs, job training, compensatory education, or treatment for depression—little systematic work has been reported about patterns and findings that cut across such program areas.

What Would Social Intervention Theory Look Like? So little work of this sort has been done, however, that good examples, or even poor ones, of what "social intervention theory" might look like are sparse. As a substitute, I will illustrate these ideas with broad suggestions about the form that social intervention theory might take.

In the context of social programs, the essential situation is one in which the program interacts with all or part of a population whose condition the program is supposed to improve through some changes the program induces. The core of any intervention theory, therefore, must be about the types of change processes actuated or facilitated by social programs and the improved conditions expected to result from that change.

Figure 1.1 provides a simple, generic diagram of these central concepts. It depicts a target population whose initial condition is such that too many individuals are below some criterion threshold on one or more dimensions of status, resources, behavior, prognosis, or the like. The concept of a threshold is useful because it recognizes the obligation of program managers and evaluators alike to identify the level at which outcomes are minimally satisfactory, and because it recognizes the natural dichotomies that are ubiquitous in social policy discourse. The group below threshold in Figure 1.1, therefore, might represent elementary students who read too far below grade level, high-risk children in dysfunctional families, substance abusers, able-bodied unemployed adults, homeless families, or a wide range of other such "social problem" situations.

Figure 1.1 also outlines the program-induced change process that is intended to yield outcome conditions in which a meaningfully large proportion of the target population has moved over the criterion threshold. Other outcomes are possible as well, including persons whose condition does not change and those who may be worse off after program intervention. Between the initial and outcome conditions, however, each individual traces a pathway in terms of whatever statuses, behaviors, situations, and the like are at issue.

Figure 1.1. Program Effects Depicted as a Change in the Proportion of a Population Above a Criterion Threshold of Well-Being

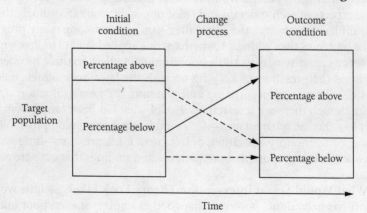

One promising way to depict the nature of those pathways and how the program intervenes to shape them is to use a version of a *stage-state* model (Runyon, 1980). In simplified form, such a model characterizes the pathway from initial to outcome conditions as a series of stages, with each individual being in some identifiable state at each stage. For instance, at the initial stage of court-ordered substance abuse treatment, a client may be in a state of denial that he or she has a substance abuse problem, or may be in a state of acceptance and admit to having a problem.

Stage-state models are relatively common in many areas of program study, though not necessarily labeled as such. Consider the case of the mass education campaign using public-service TV spots, billboards on buses, posters, and the like to promote some desirable behavior such as safe sex, low-fat diet, saying no to drugs, or whatever. The presumed stages of change induced by such programs are so well known that the model has been given a name, the KAB (knowledge, attitude, behavior) or KAP (knowledge, attitude, practice) model. It can be represented as in Figure 1.2.

In the KAB model, the media campaign is presumed to increase knowledge, which in turn affects attitude, behavioral intentions, and finally actual behavior. At each stage, we have two simple states, OK and not OK; that is, an individual either has or does not have minimally sufficient knowledge, has or does not have sufficiently positive attitudes, and so on. Because the KAB model has some generality as a model for a variety of distinct programs, it provides a small example of what intervention theory might look like. Unfortunately, it is not an encouraging model because ample evidence indicates that rather little change in behavior results from this particular intervention approach.

Another relatively well developed change model is that described by Prochaska and his colleagues (1992) for persons attempting to change addictive behavior, such as smoking, alcohol abuse, or drug abuse. Prochaska identified five general stages, shown in Figure 1.3, through which persons with addictions pass on the way to recovery, albeit with frequent backsliding. In this scheme, each stage consists essentially of one state; for example, in the precontemplation stage the addiction problem is not recognized and the client sees no need for change. There are degrees of difference, however, so some persons in this state are further along than others and closer to being ready to move to the next state/stage. This model, too, has some generality—Prochaska and his colleagues have demonstrated that it applies to a range of addictive behaviors.

Figure 1.2. The Knowledge-Attitude-Behavior (KAB) Model

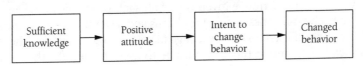

Figure 1.3. The Prochaska Addiction Recovery Model

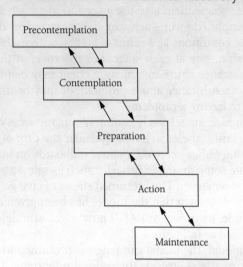

These examples, as well as others that could be presented, make the point that stage-state schemes seem especially apt for depicting generic pathways of change among program recipients. What is left out of these diagrams, however, is any representation of the program itself and how it induces movement among its clients from stage to stage. Figure 1.4 provides an expanded picture that adds the program as an organizational entity and, most importantly, the *transactions* between program and recipient that are the means by which the program attempts to shape the path of change. These transactions are shown in a *service arena* that may be offices, streets, recipients' homes, or wherever there are presumed to be potentially change-inducing interactions between program and recipient.

The critical issue for intervention theory, of course, is how many different change processes are embodied in the universe of social programs and how many different ways program activities may instigate or support them. If every program instance, or even every distinct program type, involves a unique change process and mode of interacting with recipient change pathways, little generalization will be possible. On close analysis, however, we are likely to find that beneath the surface differences there are relatively few basic change paradigms involved in social programs and a limited repertoire of program components for inducing, shaping, and supporting such change.

In a recent needs assessment, my colleagues and I developed a categorization for human service programs in Nashville (Lipsey and others, 1996) derived inductively from a descriptive inventory of all such programs in the area. We found that twelve categories of social problems and fewer than twenty categories of services were sufficient to classify a large majority of the programs. The objective of social intervention theory would be to use schemes like the diagrams

**Figure 1.4. Client Transitions Shown as a Result of
Program-Client Transactions**

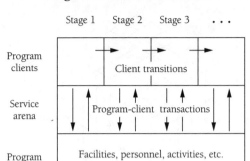

above to characterize generic categories for the different forms of human and social problems that programs address, the change paradigms the programs use (or assume) to bring about improvement in the target population, and the different program types or profiles of activities that programs organize to instigate and facilitate the change process. The result should be a rather small set of models and forms that underlie the diversity of actual program manifestations we see in the society. General social intervention theory will be found by fully identifying and describing the small set of fundamental change paradigms for social problems and the ways social programs interact with them.

Development of Intervention Theory. Though this image of intervention theory is rather abstract and sketchy, its limitations are at least in part an indication of how little systematic attention has been given to the theory-building enterprise in program evaluation research. There are several concrete steps I suggest we take to hasten the development of useful intervention theory.

Taxonomy and Classification. The first step in sorting out what we know about programs is to give appropriate attention to the matter of classification. We could make good use of our own version of the periodic table of the elements, a taxonomy that would identify and cluster similar problem conditions and the populations that experience them, basic change paradigms, and generic types of programs. It is across such clusters that we can hope to find some generalizations about the circumstances of effective and ineffective intervention. Figure 1.5 presents a simple organizational scheme we might use to begin this process.

More Explication of Program Theory in Primary Evaluation. As noted earlier, many authors have advocated that the "theory" of each program be elucidated as a framework for evaluation design and interpretation of results. It would greatly improve our information base if every evaluation routinely described the change process that was assumed in each program studied, especially if some common terminology was developed, for instance, around stage-state concepts. In addition, it would be helpful if, when possible, evaluators collected and

**Figure 1.5. Possible Structure for a Taxonomy of
Social Intervention Programs**

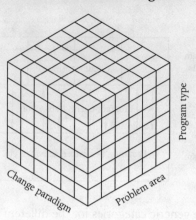

reported evidence about the pathways program recipients follow between initial and outcome conditions. This need not involve elaborate theorizing or burdensome data collection. Simply including one or two well-chosen mediating variables in the data collection and reporting their relationship to outcome could contribute importantly to our collective knowledge. Suppose, for instance, the prevailing view among the counselors in a drug prevention program you are evaluating is that the program works because it raises self-esteem and children who feel good about themselves do not use drugs. It would be informative to our emerging intervention theory, and likely to the program itself, to have the evaluation report the effects not just on drug use but also on self-esteem and how self-esteem, in turn, is related to subsequent drug use. If each evaluation included information on just one candidate mediating variable as well as the intended outcome, we would soon know much more about the pathways of change than we do now.

Dissemination. The findings of many evaluation studies are reported only to program stakeholders and are not readily available to other researchers and evaluation synthesizers. This limited dissemination places much of what we have learned in a fugitive literature and compromises any attempts at synthesis or even a full compilation of studies of a particular program type. Though it is unrealistic to expect every evaluation study to be reported in a professional journal, we need to find ways to use modern information technology to make virtually every report accessible to the evaluation community so that it might make its contribution to the cumulation of knowledge.

Meta-Analysis

Building intervention theory may be the high road to consolidating knowledge about social programs, but another route is quantitative research synthesis, or meta-analysis. A typical meta-analysis of program or treatment research will extract the statistical results of numerous studies, perhaps hundreds, and assemble them in a database along with coded information about important features of the studies producing those results. Analysis of this database can then yield generalizations about the body of research represented and the relationships within it. In this way meta-analysis helps us integrate evaluation results into a bigger picture than any one study can provide alone and is an important complement to efforts to construct broad intervention theory.

A great deal of meta-analysis of program and treatment effectiveness research has been conducted in the past two decades, and it has produced interesting and useful summaries of what we have learned in certain intervention areas. However, meta-analysis is far from realizing its full potential as a means of elucidating and integrating the cumulative knowledge embodied in the thousands of evaluation studies our field has produced. The major contribution of meta-analysis to date has been to determine the average magnitude of the effects reported across sets of similar outcome studies and compare average values for different treatment variations and types of recipients. The now classic Smith and Glass (1977) meta-analysis of psychotherapy outcome studies has been the major prototype for this work. In that meta-analysis, Smith and Glass showed that mean effect sizes did not differ greatly among different therapy types (such as psychodynamic and behavior modification), nor with major client diagnostic category (neurotic versus psychotic).

Such findings have generally been informative, albeit often controversial, for the intervention areas to which they have been applied. But although it provides useful summaries of the effects found in those areas, such meta-analysis has led to little generalization beyond the specific area of intervention to which it is applied. However, it may be possible to use meta-analysis to reveal and describe *patterns* in evaluation findings, especially those that might appear *across* as well as within different intervention areas. This might be done by applying meta-analysis to sets of studies representing multiple intervention areas, by including other forms of relevant research along with intervention studies, or by looking for generalizations across multiple meta-analyses.

The possibility that meta-analysis techniques can yield informative generalizations across broad ranges of evaluation findings and related research offers a promising approach to the task of consolidating and interpreting the body of knowledge evaluation has produced and will continue to produce. At present, however, we are talking more about potential than actual accomplishment. Nonetheless, a suggestion of the nature of the contributions that meta-analysis might make is reflected in some recent efforts my colleagues and I have undertaken that are described below.

The "Does It Work?" Issue. The common type of meta-analysis, which focuses on mean effect sizes in an intervention area, is usually attempting to determine if that intervention works and, perhaps, if some versions work better than others. For this purpose, showing that mean effect sizes are positive and significantly different from zero, or differ for different versions of the intervention, is informative. Given the hundreds of such meta-analyses that have been conducted, a simple question one might ask is how often the interventions studied seem to work. In a review of some three hundred meta-analyses of psychological, behavioral, and educational interventions, we examined the mean effect sizes reported (Lipsey and Wilson, 1993). The distribution of those mean effect sizes (in standard deviation units) was rather interesting and is shown in Figure 1.6.

What we see in Figure 1.6 is that the vast majority of the intervention areas represented showed positive mean effects. Although there are some important caveats and limitations to these results that are described in the original paper, the frequency of positive outcomes should at least give pause to those who claim that evaluators rarely find that the programs they study are effective. But here we encounter an apparent paradox: a large proportion of the individual effectiveness studies that went into these meta-analyses in fact did *not* find positive effects. That is, they did not find statistically significant differences between treatment conditions and control conditions. And yet the meta-analysis results showed an overwhelming preponderance of positive effects.

The root of this apparent inconsistency is found in a methodological problem. Individual effectiveness studies frequently have such low statistical power that they fail to reject the null hypothesis even when the observed effect is rather large. When those observed effects are averaged together in a meta-analysis, however, the aggregation is not only positive but, with the combined sample sizes of all the studies, is almost always statistically significant as well. The generalizations to be drawn are both invigorating and humbling. Our

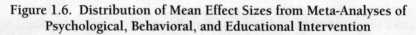

Figure 1.6. Distribution of Mean Effect Sizes from Meta-Analyses of Psychological, Behavioral, and Educational Intervention

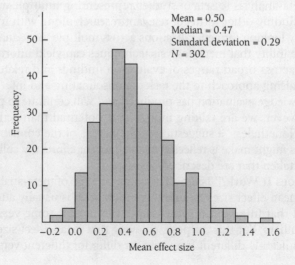

research collectively demonstrates many socially important intervention suc-
cesses, but our individual outcome studies often fail to detect meaningful
effects when they are actually there. The value of meta-analysis in this situation is that it reveals effects not otherwise observable and points the way for
methodological improvements to make outcome evaluation more sensitive to
meaningful intervention effects. This leads to an interesting side issue: the role
of method in outcome evaluation.

The Role of Method in Outcome Evaluation. Ideally our methods for
studying program effects would be like a high-quality optical lens, transmit-
ting the images of program outcomes vividly and without distortion. Another
application of meta-analysis that may help distill insight from the collective
work in evaluation is to use it to investigate not the average effects of intervention studies but the *variation* in effects across those studies. We might ask,
for instance, if that variation is mostly related to differences among studies in
the nature of the intervention, in its implementation, in the persons to whom
it was administered, and other such characteristics of the situation being studied rather than being related to methodological and procedural differences
among studies. To the extent that observed effects in evaluation studies reflect
methodological rather than substantive differences in the programs studied,
we know we are looking at them through a distorting lens, a funhouse mirror
that may make skinny effects look fat and robust effects appear anorexic.

An analysis Wilson (1995) conducted on the meta-analyses represented
in Figure 1.6 bears on this issue. Using some admittedly crude techniques, he
estimated the variance among effect sizes that was associated with the methodological and the substantive characteristics of the studies reporting those effects
in each meta-analysis. He then pooled these estimates across the three hundred meta-analyses to create the representation of effect variation shown in
Figure 1.7.

What Figure 1.7 reveals is that, for a typical intervention area, only about
one-fourth of the differences among studies in the size of the effects found by
the respective researchers can be confidently attributed to actual differences
in program characteristics. By contrast, nearly half of the variation among
observed effects is associated with sampling error and methodological differences among studies. Indeed, effect variation associated with methodological
differences is by itself nearly as large as that associated with differences among
the programs, and that associated with sampling error is slightly larger. The
implication of this analysis is that what the typical outcome study reports as
the magnitude of the intervention effect is rather approximate. Moreover, the
methodological characteristics of such studies, which are of course determined
by the researcher and the research circumstances, can have as much influence
on the observed outcome as the intervention that is supposedly being studied.

Figure 1.7 represents averaged results over a large number of intervention
areas. We might want to zoom in on the particulars of one intervention area to
determine how representative this pattern might be. One of my own meta-
analyses of outcome studies for intervention with juvenile delinquents serves

Figure 1.7. Sources of Between-Study Effect Size Variance Averaged over Three Hundred Meta-Analyses

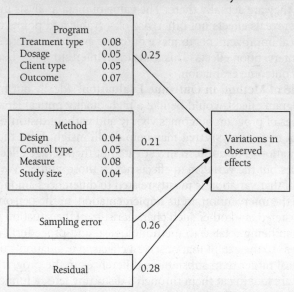

well for this purpose because it includes an unusually thorough coding of both the methodological and substantive characteristics of the available outcome studies (Lipsey, 1992). Figure 1.8 shows the variance in recidivism reduction effects associated with various sources for the four hundred studies in this meta-analysis.

The most striking feature of Figure 1.8 is how similar the results in this one intervention area are to those shown in Figure 1.7 for the average over many different intervention areas. Again we see that the characteristics of the programs themselves, which were quite diverse in this meta-analysis, accounted for less than one-fourth of the effect size variation. The method-ological differences among studies were associated with more of the effect size variance than were the between-program differences, and sampling error was larger than both.

We might think of an individual outcome study as a measurement instru-ment for intervention effects. If we translate the variance components shown in Figures 1.7 and 1.8 into an estimate of the reliability coefficient for that mea-suring instrument, it is about 0.25, the proportion of total variance associated with the characteristics of the intervention or program itself. Evaluators have long recognized that we see through a glass darkly when we are attempting to assess program effects. What meta-analysis tells us is that the glass is not only clouded, but is a distorting lens that may transmit a neither accurate nor clear image of what we are attempting to discern in our outcome studies. My con-clusion is *not* that we should refrain from conducting outcome studies but,

Figure 1.8. Sources of Between-Study Effect Size Variance in Delinquency Intervention Studies

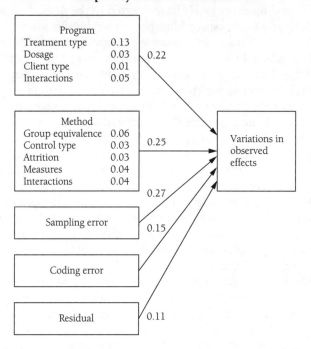

rather, that we should work steadily to improve our methods and, most importantly, that we should present the results of any one study realistically as an approximation, not a determination.

But what of the cumulation of knowledge about the nature and effects of intervention? One technique that improves the reliability of measurement is to combine multiple measures into a single, more robust composite measure, as when we add more items to an educational achievement test. If we think of each outcome study as an unreliable measure of intervention effects, we can improve reliability by combining many outcome studies and hope that, in the process, we increase the ratio of signal to noise and garner a clearer and more accurate image of program effects. This, of course, is what meta-analysis attempts to do when numbers of outcome studies are aggregated into a single analysis.

Generalizing About Intervention

As Cook (1993) has pointed out, meta-analysis is, among other things, a technique for fashioning generalizations from research. It can be used to search for and confirm patterns of results across multiple studies on a given topic. The interesting questions for this purpose have to do with the between-study differences in effect size and their relationship to the characteristics of the interventions, the clients served, the program implementation, and the like.

Cordray and Fischer (1994) have referred to the domain of differential program effects as a "policy space." Imagine a multidimensional space in which each axis represents a major manipulable characteristic of the intervention at issue. By *manipulable* I mean that program managers or policy makers could change it if they had reason to believe they would get better results that way. A most useful product of our thousands of evaluation studies would be pictures of various policy spaces that would show the combinations of program characteristics and circumstances that generated the most positive outcomes. Development of sophisticated program theory would be one way to portray such policy spaces. Meta-analysis of evaluation and related studies is another.

The following illustrates a policy space based on my meta-analysis of intervention with juvenile delinquents. For this purpose we focus only on juveniles who have engaged in violent or other very serious offenses and are treated in institutional facilities, a group of considerable concern to policymakers these days. Procedurally, we took seventy-six studies of intervention with such offenders, used a multiple regression model to control for methodological variables among the studies, and then generated the expected, or predicted, effect sizes for different interesting circumstances. Note that we relied on the actual observed effects only to build the regression model; after that, we relied on the model to construct the policy space. In this way we can try to eliminate, through statistical control, many of the distortions in the observed effects that enter because of methodological differences among studies, sampling error, and other artifacts.

This procedure shows first that one set of important variables has to do with general characteristics of the program, in particular whether it operates under juvenile justice authority (versus mental health for example), whether it uses criminal justice personnel to administer treatment, and the number of years of experience. Figure 1.9 depicts these factors. The most positive effects on recidivism appear for programs that operate outside the juvenile justice system, do not use criminal justice personnel for treatment, and have been in operation for two or more years.

If we now pick one of the program configurations shown in Figure 1.9, we can explore further the nature of successful treatment of serious, institutionalized juvenile offenders. Since most such offenders are in juvenile justice institutions, we will examine those programs, but we assume an experienced program using treatment personnel who are not agents of the criminal justice system. Figure 1.10 shows the two most important variables that are related to the outcome in these circumstances: the type of treatment provided and the integrity of the treatment implementation (that is, how fully the intended treatment is actually delivered and how closely adherence to protocol is monitored). As Figure 1.10 shows, the best effects are obtained by providing a Group I treatment with high integrity. At the other end of the spectrum, however, virtually zero effects can be expected with a Group IV treatment provided with low integrity. Intermediate between these extremes, we find a mix of useful and trivial effects.

Figure 1.9. Program Characteristics Associated with Effective Institutional Intervention for Delinquents

Youth under juvenile justice authority	Criminal justice treatment personnel	Years of program experience	Estimated mean effect size
No	No	Two or more	0.59
		Less than two	0.48
	Yes	Two or more	0.46
		Less than two	0.34
Yes	No	Two or more	0.30
		Less than two	0.18
	Yes	Two or more	0.16
		Less than two	0.05

Figure 1.10. Treatment Characteristics Associated with Effective Institutional Intervention for Delinquents

	Integrity of treatment implementation		
	Low	Medium	High
Group I Skills training Cognitive-behavioral Multiservice	0.29	0.45	0.62
Group II Counseling Drug abuse Mileau therapy Community residential	0.20	0.37	0.53
Group III Group counseling Challenge programs	0.07	0.24	0.40
Group IV Employment-related Guided group Teaching family home	0.02	0.14	0.30

This information therefore shows that the particulars of the program and intervention make a great deal of difference to the outcome. It also marshals our cumulative evaluation knowledge about programs in this area in a form that is useful to program managers and policy makers who wish to configure their programs for maximum effect. Also important, I think, is the utility of such displays of our cumulated knowledge for evaluators asked to study a program of this sort. Figures 1.8 and 1.9 provide some guidance for what effects to expect and what variables may be important in determining why those effects occur.

Conclusions

I want to finish this discussion of theory and synthesis with some simple conclusions.

1. The field of program evaluation has generated a great deal of knowledge. There is much valuable information about the nature and effects of social intervention embodied in the thousands of evaluation studies that have been conducted, but little of it is collected and integrated in ways that allow it to be used effectively.

2. Individual evaluation studies, however useful they may be to the sponsors and stakeholders, yield rather approximate estimates of intervention effects and the relationships of those effects to the features of the program under assessment. The implications of this conclusion are that there is a need for methodological improvement and that we must recognize the fallibility of the source material that serves as input to any theory-building or synthesis endeavor.

3. In the long run, our most useful and informative contribution to program managers and policy makers, and even to the evaluation profession itself, may be the consolidation of our piecemeal knowledge into broader pictures of the program and policy spaces at issue, rather than individual studies of specific programs.

4. Two promising approaches to the synthesis of what evaluation reveals about social programs are construction of social intervention theory and meta-analysis. These two are not mutually exclusive and indeed may yield the best results when used in combination. We need to find ways to support such work as part of the evaluation profession and to encourage evaluators to collect and report the data that facilitate it.

5. Kurt Lewin, the famous social psychologist, once said, "There is nothing so practical as a good theory." For program evaluators, I would amend this to say, "There is nothing so practical as a good theory *or* a good meta-analysis!"

Endnote

1. Thanks to Forscher (1963) for the brick-making metaphor.

References

Bickman, L. (ed.). *Using Program Theory in Evaluation.* New Directions for Evaluation, no. 33. San Francisco: Jossey-Bass, 1987.

Bickman, L. (ed.). *Advances in Program Theory.* New Directions for Evaluation, no. 47. San Francisco: Jossey-Bass, 1990.

Chen, H. T. *Theory-Driven Evaluation.* Newbury Park, Calif.: Sage, 1990.

Chen, H. T., and Rossi, P. H. "The Multi-Goal, Theory-Driven Approach to Evaluation: A Model Linking Basic and Applied Social Science." *Social Forces,* 1980, *59,* 106–122.

Chen, H. T., and Rossi, P. H. "Evaluating with Sense: The Theory-Driven Approach." *Evaluation Review,* 1983, *7,* 283–302.

Cook, T. D. "A Quasi-Sampling Theory of the Generalization of Causal Relationships." In L. B. Sechrest (ed.), *Understanding Causes and Generalizing About Them.* New Directions for Evaluation, no. 57, San Francisco: Jossey-Bass, 1993.

Cordray, D. S., and Fischer, R. L."Synthesizing Evaluation Findings." In J. S. Wholey, H. P. Hatry, and K. E. Newcomer (eds.), *Handbook of Practical Program Evaluation.* San Francisco: Jossey-Bass, 1994.

Forscher, B. K. "Chaos in the Brickyard." *Science,* 1963, *142,* 399.

Lipsey, M. W. "Juvenile Delinquency Treatment: A Meta-Analytic Inquiry into the Variability of Effects." In T. D. Cook, H. Cooper, D. S. Cordray, H. Hartmann, L. V. Hedges, R. J. Light, T. A. Louis, and F. Mosteller (eds.), *Meta-Analysis for Explanation: A Casebook.* New York: Russell Sage Foundation, 1992.

Lipsey, M. W. "Theory as Method: Small Theories of Treatments." In L. B. Sechrest and A. G. Scott (eds.), *Understanding Causes and Generalizing About Them.* New Directions for Program Evaluation, no. 57. San Francisco: Jossey-Bass, 1993.

Lipsey, M. W., and Pollard, J. A. "Driving Toward Theory in Program Evaluation: More Models to Choose From." *Evaluation and Program Planning,* 1989, *12,* 317–328.

Lipsey, M. W., and Wilson, D. B. "The Efficacy of Psychological, Educational, and Behavioral Treatment: Confirmation from Meta-Analysis." *American Psychologist,* 1993, *48* (12), 1181–1209.

Lipsey, M. W., Wilson, D. B., Shayne, M., Derzon, J. H., and Newbrough, J. R. "Community Needs Assessment: The Challenges of Classification and Comparison Across Diverse Needs." Research Report, Vanderbilt Institute of Public Policy Studies, 1996.

Prochaska, J. O., DiClemente, C. C., and Norcross, J. C. "In Search of How People Change: Applications to Addictive Behaviors." *American Psychologist,* 1992, *47* (9), 1102–1114.

Runyan, W. M. "A Stage-State Analysis of the Life Course." *Journal of Personality and Social Psychology,* 1980, *38* (6), 951–962.

Smith, M. L., and Glass, G. V. "Meta-Analysis of Psychotherapy Outcome Studies." *American Psychologist,* 1977, *32* (9), 752–760.

Weiss, C. H. *Evaluation Research: Methods for Assessing Program Effectiveness.* Englewood Cliffs, N.J.: Prentice Hall, 1972.

Wilson, D. B. *The Role of Method in Treatment Effect Estimates: Evidence from Psychological, Behavioral, and Educational Meta-Analyses.* Doctoral Dissertation, Claremont Graduate School, 1995.

MARK W. LIPSEY is professor in the Department of Psychology and Human Development at Vanderbilt University.

*Examining ethical questions about practice can make evaluators more
critical of what they are doing: What is it to be a good evaluator? In
whose interests should we be acting and to what purpose?*

The Landscape of Values in Evaluation: Charted Terrain and Unexplored Territory

Thomas A. Schwandt

In the past decade, issues of moral value and normative criticism in U.S. evaluation practice have risen to the foreground. The evidence here includes renewed efforts to purge evaluation of the lingering effects of the meta-theory of value-free social science (Scriven, 1991), attempts to link evaluation practice specifically to issues of social justice (House, 1993) and critical theory perspectives (Sirotnik, 1990), systematic and critical examinations of the role of values in theories of evaluation practice (Shadish, Cook, and Leviton, 1991), endorsement of standards for evaluation practice (Joint Committee on Standards for Educational Evaluation, 1994), and development and adoption of ethical principles for evaluators (Shadish, Newman, Scheirer, and Wye, 1995). Finally, discussion of the ways values influence professional evaluation practice has been a regular feature of the annual meetings of the American Evaluation Association over the past few years.

As a small contribution to this growing public discussion of the normative aims and character of evaluation practice, my purpose in this paper is to provide a descriptive and evaluative reading of values and ethics in the contemporary landscape of evaluation. Time and space do not permit a fully

---

Paper presented at the annual meeting of the American Evaluation Association, Atlanta, Georgia, November 1996. My thanks to Ernie House, Ove Karlsson, and Morten Levin for their helpful criticism of that paper. A somewhat different version of this paper, entitled "Reading the 'Problem of Evaluation' in Social Inquiry," has been published in the journal *Qualitative Inquiry*, 1997, 3 (1).

detailed examination, but I hope to provide at least an overview of major considerations.

A thoroughgoing examination of value questions is a particularly important aspect of the practice of *evaluation*. Evaluators have a special obligation to foster discussion of public moral issues as they relate to the objects they evaluate, and they are also especially obliged to submit their own practice to normative scrutiny. These responsibilities emerge from the evaluation community's claim that its expertise lies in its special knowledge of theory of evaluation. Evaluators are not simply social researchers with methodological expertise and political acumen but are obliged by the very nature of their work to make claims about the *value* of some practice, program, policy, project, or technology. Assessments of value cannot help but entail making claims about what ought to be done or avoided or what it is right to do. Judgments of value are warranted interpretations of a particular evaluand as good, good enough, poor, or corrupt (Everitt, 1996). Through making such interpretations, evaluators not only inform the means by which human or social good is realized but shape our definition of the social good as well.

Because evaluators lay claim to a special knowledge of the means and purposes of valuing, they also ought to be capable of using that expertise to evaluate their own practice. This kind of meta-evaluation includes not only assessing the worth of various methodologies (a common enough undertaking) but assessing the political morality of the practice itself. By political morality I mean the perspective in which the spheres of politics (and its issues of justice, equity, and so on) and ethics (and its issues of moral character, virtue, moral judgments, and so on) cannot be neatly decoupled in considering the purpose of a practice and the role of practitioners in the society they serve.

The Landscape of Values in Evaluation

What follows is both a descriptive and a critical reading of the landscape of ethics and values in contemporary evaluation practice. Adopting the classic anthropological stance, my aim is to give at least a partial answer to the question, What is going on here in the domain of morality and ethics?

Values as Properties or Attributes of Stakeholders' Perspectives. One of the most important lessons learned in evaluation over the past decade or so is that the practice can no longer ignore the kinds of values that are brought to policies, programs, and technologies through the actions of various stakeholders and reference groups. Evaluands are usually now not defined simply as discrete, amoral objects, devices, treatments, or interventions about which one makes simple observational claims. Rather, evaluation practice now acknowledges the fact that evaluands are social, political, and moral constructions that embody the different (and often conflicting) interests and values of stakeholders.

Evidence in support of this understanding is extensive. One of the most important contributions of nearly twenty years of work on case-study, naturalistic, and other qualitative approaches to evaluation has been that such work calls attention to the social construction of evaluands. The *Program Evaluation Standards* (Joint Committee on Standards for Educational Evaluation, 1994) have reflected this awareness since their first publication over ten years ago. The most recent strong evidence of this lesson learned is found in the statement of the fifth general principle in the *Guiding Principles for Evaluators* (Shadish, Newman, Scheirer, and Wye, 1995). That principle, labeled "Responsibilities for General and Public Welfare," reads, "Evaluators articulate and take into account the diversity of interests and values that may be related to the general and public welfare." And the first paragraph that elaborates on that principle states, "When planning and reporting evaluations, evaluators should consider including important perspectives and interests of the full range of stakeholders in the object being evaluated."

Of course, it remains a matter of much debate about how best to undertake the task of including stakeholder values in an evaluation—that is, *how* to identify stakeholders' understandings of the intrinsic, instrumental, and contributory worth of evaluands, and, once such an identification is made, what to do with that information in the assessment of the value of the evaluand. However, it is no longer a question of *whether* we should make such an examination.

Values as Applied Ethics: Professional Conduct. The field of evaluation has made great strides in the past ten years in recognizing and promoting this aspect of applied ethics. After extensive discussion at the annual meetings and considerable work on the part of a special task force, the membership of American Evaluation Association endorsed the *Guiding Principles for Evaluators*. These principles are not specific rules for conduct nor codified as something to which evaluators must take an oath of allegiance. They are guidelines, not standards. Yet that does not diminish their importance; there are many professional practices that have codes of conduct or sets of ethical principles of this sort. Nor does it matter that the scope and depth of the coverage of these principles are disputed, for they are mainly intended to raise awareness of ethical conduct in practice and stimulate debate, not to monitor or sanction individual practitioners. What does matter is that the principles are evidence of a community of evaluation practitioners searching for ideals of right conduct, including, but also extending beyond, the usual concern for methodological matters.

This is a critically important activity because the common moral condition, the activity of being a moral self, is incurably, inherently ambivalent. In other words, the moral life is not plagued by an ambiguity and tentativeness that must somehow be eradicated or overcome by the discovery of the principles or foundations of morality. Rather, to live a moral life is by definition a matter of human interaction and thus bears all the characteristics of the messiness and uncertainty of human existence—emotion, intuition, decisions about how to relate perceptual knowledge to standing commitments, and the like. Zygmunt Bauman (1993) captures this conclusion:

The probable truth is that moral choices are indeed choices, and dilemmas are indeed dilemmas—not the temporary and rectifiable effects of human weakness, ignorance or blunders. Issues have no predetermined solutions nor have the cross-roads intrinsically preferable predetermined directions. There are no hard-and-fast principles which one can learn, memorize and deploy in order to escape situations without a good outcome and to spare oneself the bitter after taste . . . which comes unsolicited in the wake of decisions taken and fulfilled. Human reality is messy and ambiguous—and so moral decisions, unlike abstract ethical principles, are ambivalent. It is in this sort of world that we must live; and yet, as if defying the worried philosophers who cannot conceive of an 'unprincipled' morality, a morality without foundations, we demonstrate day by day that we can live, or learn to live, or manage to live in such a world, though few of us would be ready to spell out, if asked, what the principles that guide us are, and fewer still would have heard about the 'foundations' which we allegedly cannot do without to be good and kind to each other. (p. 32)

In sum, morality quite literally means accepting the reality of the vicissitudes of human life as we try to create, maintain, and enhance positive relations with others. Morality means cultivating moral recognition and awareness, learning to develop normative attentiveness, understanding how virtues such as honesty and trust apply in concrete encounters with others, wrestling with never very tidy moral decisions that almost always leave moral remainders. In this perspective, morality is not about solving problems in ways of relating to one another but about facing mysteries and dilemmas that demand practical-moral wisdom (May, 1991). It means not turning what is essentially a hermeneutic situation into a technical problem and viewing it with objective detachment. Rather, moral knowledge is something that is enacted and hence guided by understanding of the specific circumstance. Codes, principles, and general moral rules are indeed available to us, but they are secondary to and sensible only in light of the particulars of concrete cases, and concrete cases are marked by ambiguity and finiteness of understanding.

Values as Applied Ethics: Values as Relevant Subject Matter in Evaluation. Applied ethics also encompasses the question of whether (and which) values are relevant subject matter in evaluating the goals, operation, and outcomes of policies, programs, projects, and technologies (Scriven, 1991). This concern now seems to be firmly planted on the professional agenda, and the debate involves two issues.

The first issue has to do with identifying and defining the relevant set of absolute and practical values bearing on the evaluand. Consider, for example, a program designed to provide in-home health care to physically disabled individuals. What absolute values are important here: fairness and equity in services provided? Absence of any additional harm in the act of providing the service? And what practical values are important: efficiency? Physical appearance of health care personnel? Or consider a case of evaluating the ethical conduct of the evaluator: What set of absolute and practical values should be brought to bear here? The story of the controversy surrounding the inclusion in the *Guiding Principles* of the fifth principle, "Responsibilities for General and Public Welfare" (which holds that the evaluator's obligations extend beyond meeting clients' needs and encompass the public interest and good; Shadish, Newman, Scheier, and Wye, 1995) illustrates the struggle to identify an absolute value—in this case, the ethical obligation to consider the public good—and points to the difficulty of identifying relevant absolute values and warranting their inclusion in an evaluation.

The second issue concerns defining what it means to take such values into account in making an evaluative judgment. In other words, let us suppose an evaluator is successful in identifying relevant absolute and practical values related to justice, equity, respect for persons, and so forth in the circumstances of a particular evaluation. Then the question becomes, What to do with those values? Here, traditionally, we have two answers, reflecting considerable disagreement on the moral proposition that the evaluator ought to be making summative value judgments.

One answer claims that an evaluator simply is not engaging in the activity of evaluating if he or she does not consider all relevant values bearing on the performance of the evaluand and does not subsequently render a summative judgment based on those values. These values function as criteria for judging the merit of the evaluand. They are taken into account through a variety of means, including needs assessments, logical analysis of the function of an evaluand, and careful argumentation for those general ethical principles that, in part, constitute the sociopolitical context in which the evaluand was conceived and in which the activity of evaluation unfolds.

The second answer disagrees. It admits that it is insufficient simply to generate factual data about the performance of an evaluand and that value-related data must be uncovered as well. However, it argues that no value judgment based on a synthesis of all these data should actually be forthcoming from the evaluator. This position asserts that the *evaluator* must not make a value judgment based on consideration of relevant absolute and practical values. Rather, the evaluator should describe the various values held by stakeholders or show how different value perspectives may lead to different conclusions about the merit or worth of the evaluand. It is the responsibility of primary stakeholders to make the final judgment of the merit of the evaluand (Shadish, 1994). The defense of this position appears to rest on at least two claims. The first is that the evaluator cannot make warranted claims about the value of an evaluand because there is no generally agreed-on moral theory that supplies the justification for particular moral claims. Rather, we have a proliferation of moral theories (such as various theories of justice as defined, for example, by Locke, Kant, and more recently Rawls; theories of virtue as advanced by neo-Aristotelians such as MacIntyre; feminist ethical theories of care as defended by Noddings or trust as explained by Baier), no one of which is regarded as clearly superior. But there is a serious flaw in this argument: the debate over which is the best moral theory or which theory provides the best justification for particular moral claims need not be settled before we can identify what has moral value and make justified moral judgments. That would be equivalent to saying we cannot engage in the activity of relating in meaningful ways to others in society until we first have agreement on the best theory of society. The same empirically well-supported moral claims—that one should always help those in need, that honesty in one's dealings with other people is good, that safety is an absolute requirement in children's toys, and so on—are compatible with but receive different justifications in different moral theories.

A second argument given in support of the descriptive valuing position is this: when the evaluator is specifically charged with making a value judgment, it is likely that the evaluator's values will become the basis for the judgment. But this conclusion is not necessarily derivable from its premises. Values as criteria can come from many sources, but they need not (and should not) arise from the evaluator's personal tastes or preferences. To be sure, evaluators are typically citizens in the same society wherein an evaluand is being examined. In this way, the identification of relevant values is, in some way, admitting that the evaluator-as-citizen personally holds the values shared by all citizens in the society. But said values are not the property of the evaluator's individual personal taste nor are commonly held values somehow the sum or average of the values held by all individuals. Rather, values are intersubjective—that is, they are part of what constitutes the life-world of which the evaluator-evaluand-stakeholders are all a part. What the evaluator is doing in identifying values and basing a judgment of program merit on shared values evident in needs analyses, cost analyses, and so on is making an interpretative justification (Fraser, 1989).

Values in the Application of Evaluations. At issue here are the standard moral questions stemming from external political pressures on the work of evaluators as well as the applications made of evaluation knowledge. There is a substantial body of work spanning two decades that reflects on these kinds of moral questions. It includes the work of Lee Cronbach on the fit of evaluation to systems of accommodation versus command; Carol Weiss's extensive work on the politics of evaluation; Daniel Stufflebeam and William Webster's efforts to distinguish pseudo from legitimate evaluations; the work of Barry MacDonald and others in the CARE group on democratic evaluation; and, most recently, Eleanor Chelimsky's concerns for protecting the independence of evaluators in the political arena by taking steps to guard against the evaluator's vulnerability to partisan attack. Of course, this part of the landscape also includes current concerns about the moral stances of partisanship, value neutrality, and advocacy in evaluation, as evidenced, for example, in the recent exchange between Daniel Stufflebeam and David Fetterman over the matter of empowerment evaluation (Fetterman, 1994, 1995; Stufflebeam, 1994). But this really is the stuff of the following dimension.

Values Constituting the Ethical Aim of Evaluation. At issue here is the question of the moral end in view or the human or social good that evaluation practice is intended to serve. This is a question of the political morality of the practice and, in my judgment, the least understood and the least examined part of the portrait I am sketching. This is so because most answers to the question, To what purpose or in whose interest should evaluation practice be conducted?, are given in epistemological or political terms. But there are ethical claims at stake in answers to this question as well—claims about the nature of the moral life, claims about agency, authority, identity and human interaction, claims about the way society ought to be and the ways professionals ought to serve that society, and so forth. In other words, there is an important sense in which a morality is wedded to epistemology and politics (Taylor, 1987). The remainder of this paper is devoted to exploring three ways in which this union is conceived, using a set of terms introduced by Rein (1983) in his examination of policy studies. I begin by describing an ethics for social inquiry that, paradoxically, claims to keep epistemology and political morality distinct by maintaining an amoral, apolitical stance. Then I discuss an emancipatory ethical aim, and finally the ethical aim of fostering practical wisdom. What I am about to discuss is something like ideal types that various kinds of practices of evaluation aspire to. These types do not comprise a template by which practices can be neatly sorted, and above all they do not map onto the so-called qualitative-quantitative debate in evaluation methodology.

An Analytical, Value-Neutral Framework. In this conception of the ethical aim of the practice, the purpose of evaluation is to generate a particular kind of social scientific knowledge that can be used to ameliorate social problems. The moral claim made here is that in generating that knowledge, evaluation practice ought to be neutral with respect to the ways in which that knowledge can be used to serve different ends that society values. In other words, the knowledge produced in professional evaluation should be principally empirical, not normative. The evaluator qua social scientist has no business making evaluative conclusions; he or she should be disinterested and, in that sense, value neutral with respect to different conceptions of a good program, a good society, and so on. Social inquirers can describe various value positions held by members of society, but they should never engage in judging which is the best. This is necessary, the argument goes, because while reason is a valuable guide to adjudicating claims about matters of empirical fact, it is useless for deciding among competing values.

This framework for defining evaluation practice is most evident in the fact-gathering, or monitoring, approach to evaluation as well as in the descriptive valuing approach, including what Scriven (1993) calls the "weak decision support" and the "relativistic" views of evaluation. It derives from the Weberian and Mertonian claim to a "disinterested" or value-free social science (Merton, 1973) and is predicated on what Weber (1963) called the "unbridgeable distinction" between the work of the social scientist and the work of the ordinary, evaluating, acting person:

> To apply the results of this (scientific) analysis in the making of a decision is not a task which science can undertake; it is rather the task of the acting, willing

person: he [sic] weighs and chooses from among the values involved according
to his own conscience and his personal view of the world. Science can make
him realize that all action, and naturally . . . inaction, imply in their consequences the espousal of certain values and . . . the rejection of certain others.
The act of choice itself is his own responsibility. (p. 359)

Various defenses of this position have been made over the years, and the strong
critique of this view as an inappropriate meta-theory for evaluation (Scriven,
1993) and social inquiry in general (Bernstein, 1976; Hollis, 1994; Root, 1993)
is well known.

Paradoxically, this framework claims to be amoral; that is, it has no moral
aim other than upholding the view that the good of society is best served by
the production of valid, reliable information on the part of social inquirers.
Though not indifferent to the idea of improving society or social life, this
framework is based on the belief that that goal is best accomplished by clearly
limiting the expertise of the professional social inquirer to empirical matters.
In fact, in empirical matters, the authority of the inquirer is regarded as (relatively) absolute because of the special knowledge he or she possesses about
methodology. The ethic of this perspective is principally scientific. It is an ethic
concerned with what counts as responsible behavior in the generation and
analysis of data. It is an ethic that governs not *engagement with* but *disengage-
ment from* the normal, customary flow of partisan, emotive, subjective meaning schemes that characterize human interaction and social life generally
(Sievers, 1983).

As a stance toward society, the analytical framework defines social problems in an apolitical, scientific manner. Social policy is seen more or less as an
exercise in social technology. Karl Popper's idea of piecemeal social engineering is perhaps the most famous expression of this framework. In program evaluation, this theory of practice is most evident in Donald Campbell's (1969,
1982) notion of the experimenting society. More recent explanations of this
framework emphasize that the social scientist must be politically astute in
understanding ways in which scientific information can be fed into the policy
making process. Carol Weiss (1983, 1987), for example, has been particularly
concerned with how social scientists and evaluators introduce their empirical
work into the mix of interest, ideologies, and information characterizing the
policy environment. Her belief is that social scientific information can be introduced into the mix to help resolve conflicts in ideologies and interests. In this
way, evaluation knowledge is less likely to be directly or instrumentally applied
but rather used to enlighten policy makers and program planners.

Arguably, this theory of the political morality of the practice of evaluation
(and social science practice more broadly) is the most dominant framework in
the West. It has served both the utilitarian, technocratic conception of democracies that was prominent in the 1960s and 1970s as well as the more recent
versions of pluralist-elitist-equilibrium theories of democracy (House, 1993).
It has become virtually a background ideology that dictates both the under-

standing of social problems and the knowledge required to solve them. To borrow a turn of phrase from Sullivan (1983), in this ideology, social scientists aspire to be something like scientific shepherds who lead or at least wish they led a highly rationalized flock. In contemporary defenses of this analytical framework in evaluation practice, one hears at least an implied lament that scientific rationality must always regrettably cope with the messy world of political rationality.

In the United States, this theory of practice has been fairly comfortably allied with economic and social laissez faire approaches to the polity. Its defenders claim they are acting in the service of individual freedom, providing information that makes the marketplace of ideas a more secure—that is, rational—place in which competing interests can bargain. As Shadish recently observed, evaluation informed by this theory of practice "serves a system-enhancing role" by "giving all stakeholders the information they need to fight their battles in the political and social arena" (1996, p. 4).

On the horizon it seems likely that this framework for evaluation practice will complement the new mangerialism arising across the West that seeks to transform the culture of public services through devolution and decentralization (Clarke, Cochrane, and McLaughlin, 1994; Pollitt, 1995). This is paradoxical, because the new managerialism, in part, grows out of a reaction against the authority of professionals to direct social problem identification and treatment. The movement (if that is the correct term) emphasizes depoliticizing social policy, going beyond national political debates to produce rational and efficient decisions about the deployment of social resources at local levels. This avowedly apolitical character, coupled with a strong interest in allegedly neutral criteria of economy, efficiency, and effectiveness, is likely to make the new managerialism resonate strongly with the analytical, value-neutral perspective in social inquiry. The difference will be that social scientists and evaluators will turn away from serving the state, with its messy partisan world that makes use of scientific information difficult, to serving the needs of managers.

An Emancipatory, Value-Committed Framework. The analytical, value-neutral framework arose out of sustained criticism of inherited, unquestioned authority. It championed the critical scrutiny of empirical evidence to reach reasoned conclusions about appropriate possible courses of social action. The value-committed framework arises largely out of criticisms that the analytical, value-neutral framework has lost its emancipatory, liberatory, and democratic origins. The familiar argument is that the analytical framework with its goal of enlightening policy makers has become wedded to a cognitive-instrumental-technical outlook, lacks a critical purchase, and has become a rationale for an elitist science that serves existing structures of power. Evaluation informed by a value-committed framework also seeks a particular kind of scientific knowledge. However, this knowledge is not at all disinterested.

Although there are important differences among value-committed frameworks grounded in participatory, feminist, and critical science perspectives, all share a view of human agency at odds with the analytical, value-neutral framework. Value-committed perspectives take political rationality as the primary starting point or arena for conceiving of evaluation practice. Negotiation, conflict, and ideological struggle is the stuff with which evaluation practice must come to terms. But this does not mean that evaluation is conceived solely in terms of political rhetoric. Rather, it signals a different ethic of engagement. The value-neutral, analytic perspective on evaluation practice emphasizes breaking from ordinary interactive relationships in favor of scientific rationality, nonpartisanship, and neutrality with respect to ethical values embedded in human actions (such as policies, projects, programs) that are under examination. In contrast, emancipatory practices seek to be continuous with human interaction and reflect a commitment to everyday life. Flacks summarizes this commitment as follows: "A morally guided social science must have the goal of enabling people themselves to make their own history, of breaking down the structures and motivational frameworks that sustain elitism and privatism, of achieving social arrangements in which communities can engage in the formulation of the terms and conditions of daily life as an integral part of daily life itself" (1983, p. 349). Giddens explains that the central ethic of emancipatory approaches is to "liberate individuals and groups from constraints adversely affecting their life chances" (1991, p. 210). He argues that the political morality of emancipatory inquiry is best characterized as (a) a politics of others—it is concerned with division between human beings made on the basis of class, gender, ethnicity, ruling versus subordinate, rich versus poor, and so on; (b) concerned with power and the reduction or elimination of exploitation, inequality, and oppression in social relations; and (c) having the primary imperatives of justice, equality, and participation.

There are many variations of evaluation practice that share this general framework, and they differ widely on what precisely the emancipatory end in view is and on the way it should be achieved or enacted. In a recent paper, for example, Mertens (1995) argues from a feminist perspective that evaluation practice ought to recognize silence or marginalized voices, analyze power inequities, and be linked to political action. Although not sharing all these assumptions of so-called emancipatory evaluation, House's (1993) arguments for evaluation practice in service of social justice share an emancipatory aim. He argues that value neutrality must be replaced by the bid to search out and give special consideration to the views and interests of minority stakeholders. Approaches to evaluation practice informed by neo-Marxist critical theory likewise reflect an emancipatory aim (Sirotnik and Oakes, 1990). These practices emphasize that a program evaluation should be designed in relationship to and provide an understanding of the broader sociopolitical and economic context in which the program unfolds, explicitly embrace the stance of social justice, and ameliorate unjust social conditions (Richardson, 1990).

A Value-Critical Framework. This framework shares with the value-committed approach an emphasis on the primacy of everyday life and a skepticism toward goal-rational solutions to social problems. It also shares a belief with both value-neutral and value-committed frameworks in the possibility of improving the rationality of human practices. But it differs sharply in its view of the nature and aim of social inquiry and the role that professional inquiry plays in clarifying and shaping the contours of social discourse. Evaluation practices guided by value-neutral and value-committed frameworks endeavor to keep professional social inquiry at or near the center of social life (Lindbloom, 1990). They do so in two ways: first, by defining that which is to be evaluated as an object *about which* knowledge is to be generated by professional inquiry, and second, by defining social research as a systematic, methodical process for acquiring positive knowledge of these objects that can, in turn, be used to direct society. Although the notion of a scientifically guided society is certainly the strongest in the analytical perspective, scientific social inquiry also plays a crucial role in emancipatory practices in helping members of society see how they have been wrong-headed, misguided, unclear, or even delusional in their policies, practices, and technologies.

In contrast, evaluation practices based in a value-critical framework decenter this conception of the aim, nature, and place of social inquiry in social life. They do so by redefining social inquiry as a dialogical and reflective process of democratic discussion and philosophical critique (Carr, 1995). A value-critical perspective abandons the nearly exclusive preoccupation of social inquiry with generating methodical (that is, method-driven) knowledge *about* the rationality of human practices (projects, programs, policies). It does not regard what is to be evaluated as an object about which theoretical knowledge must be generated. Rather, what is evaluated is a human practice or action in which human beings are engaged. The activity of producing social knowledge of objects through the application of method is replaced with a conception of social inquiry aimed at cultivating practical wisdom that in turn is not *about* the practice but constitutive of the practice itself. In this way, a value-critical framework removes professional social inquiry from the center of society and replaces it with a focus on praxis and the cultivation of practical wisdom.

Improving praxis by enabling practitioners to refine the rationality of their practices is the aim of evaluation conducted in a value-critical framework. This can only be achieved by helping practitioners develop a kind of educative, critically reflective self-knowledge that enables them to question the beliefs and unstated assumptions that sustain a particular practice of education, management, social service, health care, and so forth (Carr, 1995; Pendlebury, 1995). Human endeavors such as educating, managing, providing health care and social services, and so forth are constructed around standing commitments to what is good and right; they are oriented toward agreed-on social aims. At the same time, these endeavors or practices are essentially characterized by their mutability, indeterminacy, and particularity, which make it impossible to use systems of general rules and principles to judge their goodness. Judging the merit of a particular practice (that is, whether it is good, good enough, poor, or corrupt) thus requires cultivating perceptual awareness of concrete particulars. Yet one cannot ignore standing commitments and general principles that form the traditions of various practices. Nor, because of the mutability and indeterminacy of practices, can we engage in some process of weighing alternative goals, values, criteria, and the like that reduces judgment of what constitutes good practice to calculation. Rather, we must engage in strong evaluation, judging the qualitative worth of the different aims of our practices by bringing into simultaneous critical examination the perceptual knowledge of the concrete details of a practice and the conceptual knowledge of principles that have traditionally shaped the goods of that practice (Pendlebury, 1995).

The notion of evaluation expertise is not abandoned in this undertaking. In some ways it is actually enhanced, for it means teaching *about* what it means to engage in a kind of evaluation that is constitutive of the exercise of practical-moral judgment. The difference is that the evaluators use their special knowledge about what it means to evaluate and how to come to warranted conclusions of the worth of human practices to *add to* and encourage practitioners' reflective, conversational critiques of the value commitments embedded in their practices. An evaluator's knowledge is used in a complementary or supplementary manner. It is not knowledge in the form of a pronouncement about an evaluation object from an allegedly detached, objective, and disinterested observer who enlightens practitioners or seeks to emancipate them from the chains of false consciousness, erroneous reason, and the like. Nor is it knowledge in the form of partisan concern for local narratives and local attention to fine-grained particularities of practice. Rather it is a kind of knowledge that supplements or complements the knowledge of practitioners. Evaluation practices informed by this ethic of cultivating practical wisdom thus take different pedagogical forms than practices characterized by enlightenment and emancipatory aims (Schwandt, 1996, 1997). Examples include the dialogue conferences characteristic of some forms of Scandinavian action research and the modeling of evaluation on Socratic dialogues (Eldin and Levine, 1991; Gustavsen, 1992; Karlsson, 1995).

In summary, what I have sketched here are three different ways of conceiving of the ethical aim of evaluation practice. To argue that one's aim is to enlighten, to emancipate, or to cultivate practical wisdom is not simply to make a cognitive claim—that is, a defense of a particular kind of evaluation knowledge or a particular way of warranting an evaluation claim. It is also to take an ethical stance on the question of how one ought to *be* as an evaluator in society and to make a claim about the goods or ends served by the particular human practice we call evaluation.

Conclusion

The point of this brief portrait of the ways in which ethics and values are manifest in evaluation practice is really a quite simple one, yet perhaps a very profound one. Ethical discussion aims at making us more critical of what we are doing. It brings us back to thinking about what it is to be a good evaluator, and to asking, In whose interests should we be acting, and to what purpose?

These are ethical questions, and they should take precedence over technical questions of how to *do* evaluation. They take precedence in the sense that they are an indispensable requirement for any genuinely educational science such as evaluation. To paraphrase an observation by Carr (1995, p. 99), it is only by virtue of a self-conscious desire to be guided and informed by philosophical beliefs about the value of a particular practice that the educational character of that practice can be recognized and sustained. This concern with the primacy of ethical questions in understanding (and reforming) a social practice is not a kind of philosophical or moral imperialism, as Patton (1997) has recently charged. Rather, it is an acknowledgment that the assumed neutrality of technique does not allow us to escape difficult questions about the moral and political meaning of our practice for the society in which we work.

The social science legacy of evaluation practice is undeniable; it cannot be undone. But what can be done is to recognize the limitations on conceptions of evaluation practice imposed by that tradition. Perhaps the greatest limitation is that we are easily convinced that what matters most about what it means to do good evaluation is which model, method, or methodology we should use or whether evaluation is best conceived as utilization-focused, objectivist, naturalistic, or quasi-experimental. We ought not to let these concerns overwhelm ethics in the conception of our practice. And that, of course, is itself a moral claim.

References

Bauman, Z. *Postmodern Ethics.* Oxford: Blackwell, 1993.

Bernstein, R. J. *Restructuring Social and Political Theory.* Philadelphia: University of Pennsylvania Press, 1976.

Campbell, D. T. "Reforms as Experiments." *American Psychologist,* 1969, *24,* 409–429.

Campbell, D. T. "Experiments as Arguments." In E. R. House, S. Mathison, J. A. Pearsol, and H. Preskill (eds.), *Evaluation Studies Review Annual,* Vol. 7. Beverly Hills, Calif.: Sage, 1982.

Carr, W. *For Education: Towards Critical Educational Inquiry.* Buckingham, U.K.: Open University Press, 1995.

Clarke, J., Cochrane, A., and McLaughlin, E. (eds.). *Managing Social Policy.* London: Sage, 1994.

Eldin, M., and Levine, M. Cogenerative Learning. In W. F. Whyte (ed.), *Participatory Action Research.* Newbury Park, Calif.: Sage, 1991.

Everitt, A. "Developing Critical Evaluation." *Evaluation,* 1006, *2* (2), 173–188.

Fetterman, D. "Empowerment Evaluation." *Evaluation Practice,* 1994, *15* (1), 1–15.

Fetterman, D. "In Response." *Evaluation Practice,* 1995, *16* (2), 179–199.

Flacks, R. "Moral Commitment, Privatism, and Activism: Notes on a Research Program." In N. Hann, R. N. Bellah, P. Rabinow, and W. Sullivan (eds.), *Social Science as Moral Inquiry.* New York: Columbia University Press, 1983.

Fraser, N. (1989). "Talking About Needs: Interpretive Contests as Political Conflicts in Welfare State Societies." *Ethics,* 1989, *99,* 291–313.

Giddens, A. *Modernity and Self-Identity.* Cambridge, U.K.: Polity Press, 1991.

Gustavsen, B. (1992). *Dialogue and Development.* Maastricht, the Netherlands: Van Gorcum, 1992.

Hollis, M. *The Philosophy of Social Science.* Cambridge, U.K.: Cambridge University Press, 1994.

House, E. R. *Professional Evaluation*. Newbury Park, Calif.: Sage, 1993.

Joint Committee on Standards for Educational Evaluation. *Program Evaluation Standards*. (2nd ed.) Thousand Oaks, Calif.: Sage, 1994.

Karlsson, O. "How Can the Interaction Between Evaluation and Politics Be Tackled?" Paper presented at the First International Evaluation Conference, Vancouver, British Columbia, Nov. 1995.

Lindbloom, C. E. *Inquiry and Change*. New Haven, Conn.: Yale University Press, 1990.

May, W. F. *The Patients' Ordeal*. Bloomington: Indiana University Press, 1991.

Mertens, D. "Identifying and Respecting Differences Among Participants in Evaluation Studies." In W. R. Shadish, D. L. Newman, M. A. Scheirer, and C. Wye (eds.), *Guiding Principles for Evaluators*. New Directions for Program Evaluation, no. 66. San Francisco: Jossey-Bass, 1995.

Merton, R. *The Sociology of Science: Theoretical and Empirical Investigations*. Chicago: University of Chicago Press, 1973.

Patton. M. Q. *Utilization-Focused Evaluation*. (3rd ed.) Thousand Oaks, Calif.: Sage, 1997.

Pendlebury, S. "Reason and Story in Wise Practice." In H. McEwan and K. Egan (eds.), *Narrative in Teaching, Learning and Research*. New York: Teachers College Press, 1995.

Pollitt, C. "Justification by Works or Faith? Evaluating the New Public Management." *Evaluation*, 1995, *1* (2), 133–154.

Rein, M. *From Policy to Practice*. London: Macmillan, 1983.

Richardson, V. "At-Risk Programs: Evaluation as Critical Inquiry." In K. A. Sirotnik (ed.), *Evaluation and Social Justice: Issues in Public Education*. New Directions for Program Evaluation, no. 45. San Francisco: Jossey-Bass, 1990.

Root, M. *Philosophy of Social Scence*. Oxford: Blackwell, 1993.

Schwandt, T. A. "Farewell to Criteriology." *Qualitative Inquiry*, 1996, *2* (1), 58–72.

Schwandt, T. A. "Evaluation as Practical Hermeneutics." *Evaluation*, 1997, *5* (1), 69–83.

Scriven, M. *Evaluation Thesaurus*. (4th ed.) Newbury Park, Calif.: Sage, 1991.

Scriven, M. (ed.). *Hard-Won Lessons in Program Evaluation*. New Directions for Program Evaluation, no. 58. San Francisco: Jossey-Bass, 1993.

Shadish, W. R. "Need-Based Evaluation Theory: What Do You Need to Know to Do Good Evaluation?" *Evaluation Practice*, 1994, *15* (3), 347–358.

Shadish, W. R. "Descriptive Values and Social Justice." *Evaluation Theories* (newsletter of the Topical Interest Group in Evaluation Theory), 1996, *4* (1), 1–5.

Shadish, W. R., Cook, T. D., and Leviton, L. *Foundations of Program Evaluation: Theories of Practice*. Newbury Park, Calif.: Sage, 1991.

Shadish, W. R., Newman, D. L., Scheirer, M. A., and Wye, C. (eds.). (1995). *Guiding Principles for Evaluators*. New Directions for Program Evaluation, no. 66. San Francisco: Jossey-Bass, 1995.

Sievers, B. "Believing in Social Science: The Ethics and Epistemology of Public Opinion Research." In N. Haan, R. N. Bellah, P. Rabinow, and W. Sullivan (eds.), *Social Science as Moral Inquiry*. New York: Columbia University Press, 1983.

Sirotnik, K. A. (ed.). *Evaluation and Social Justice: Issues in Public Education*. New Directions for Program Evaluation, no. 45. San Francisco: Jossey-Bass, 1990.

Sirotnik, K. A. and Oakes, J. "Evaluation as Critical Inquiry: School Improvement as a Case in Point." In K. A. Sirotnik (ed.), *Evaluation and Social Justice: Issues in Public Education*. New Directions for Program Evaluation, no. 45. San Francisco: Jossey-Bass, 1990.

Stufflebeam, D. L. "Empowerment Evaluation, Objectivist Evaluation, and Evaluation Standards: Where the Future of Evaluation Should Not Go and Where It Needs to Go." *Evaluation Practice*, 1994, *15* (3), 321–338.

Sullivan, W. M. "Beyond Policy Science: The Social Sciences as Moral Sciences." In N. Haan, R. N. Bellah, P. Rabinow, and W. Sullivan (eds.), *Social Science as Moral Inquiry*. New York: Columbia University Press, 1983.

Taylor, C. "Overcoming Epistemology." In K. Baynes, J. Bohman, and T. McCarthy (eds.), *After Philosophy: End or Transformation?* Cambridge, Mass.: MIT Press, 1987.

Weber, M. "Objectivity in Social Science and Social Policy." In M. Natanson (ed.), *Philoso-phy of the Social Sciences.* New York: Random House, 1963.

Weiss, C. "Ideology, Interest, and Information: The Basis of Policy Decisions." In D. Calla-han and B. Jennings (eds.), *Ethics, Social Sciences, and Policy Analysis.* New York: Plenum, 1983.

Weiss, C. "The Circuitry of Enlightenment." *Knowledge: Creation, Diffusion, Utilization,* 1987, *8,* 274–281.

THOMAS A. SCHWANDT is associate professor of education at Indiana University and coordinator of the Educational Inquiry Methodology Program, Bloomington, Indiana.

Theory-based evaluation examines conditions of program implementation and mechanisms that mediate between processes and outcomes as a means to understand when and how programs work.

Theory-Based Evaluation: Past, Present, and Future

Carol H. Weiss

Theory-based evaluation has surged to attention in recent years. Evaluators are writing about it, and evaluations structured around theory are beginning to appear in numbers in the literature.

The Past

The concept of theory-based evaluation has been around for over twenty-five years. In the spring–summer 1996 issue *Evaluation Practice* published two early papers—an excerpt from my 1972 book *Evaluation Research* and Fitz-Gibbon and Morris (1975)—along with a historical introduction by Blaine Worthen (1996). I have been trying to go back further. In his 1967 book *Evaluative Research,* Edward Suchman referred several times to the notion of programs' theories. Suchman discussed two kinds of reasons for an unsuccessful program: failure of the program to put the intended activities into operation (implementation failure) and failure of the activities to bring about the desired effects (theory failure). My 1972 book offered the first discussion Worthen and I have found of the central idea of basing evaluation on the program's theory. I included a diagram of several alternative theories on which a program of teachers' home visiting might be based. See Figure 3.1. I called the subject a "process model," and I urged that the evaluator collect data on the posited links.

In succeeding years there were a few papers on the subject. Joe Wholey's work on evaluability assessment stressed the need to find out whether the implicit theory underlying a program made sense (Wholey 1979, 1983). Wholey's idea was that prior to the start of a formal study, the evaluator

NEW DIRECTIONS FOR EVALUATION, no. 76, Winter 1997 © Jossey-Bass Publishers

Figure 3.1. Theory of a Program of Teacher Home Visits

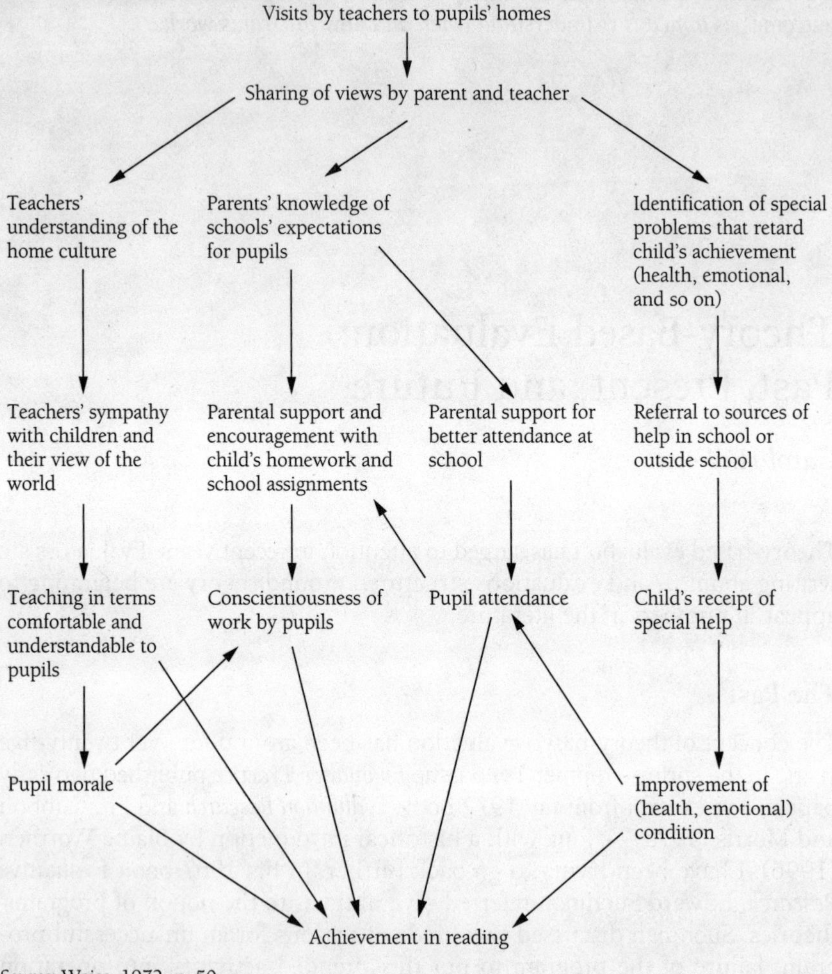

Visits by teachers to pupils' homes

Sharing of views by parent and teacher

Teachers' understanding of the home culture

Parents' knowledge of schools' expectations for pupils

Identification of special problems that retard child's achievement (health, emotional, and so on)

Teachers' sympathy with children and their view of the world

Parental support and encouragement with child's homework and school assignments

Parental support for better attendance at school

Referral to sources of help in school or outside school

Teaching in terms comfortable and understandable to pupils

Conscientiousness of work by pupils

Pupil attendance

Child's receipt of special help

Pupil morale

Improvement of (health, emotional) condition

Achievement in reading

Source: Weiss, 1972, p. 50.

should analyze the logical reasoning that connected program inputs to desired outcomes to see whether there was a reasonable likelihood that goals could be achieved.

Huey-Tsyh Chen and Peter Rossi discussed the idea in a series of publications (Chen and Rossi, 1980, 1983, 1987; Chen, 1990, 1994). Their addition to the discussion included the idea that the theory should be a social science theory, not just a series of ad hoc logical premises. Chen (1990) also distinguished between normative theory and causal theory. Normative theory "provides guidance on what goals and outcomes should be pursued or examined" (p. 43), whereas causal theory was the set of assumptions about how the program works. Causal theory is what most of the previous authors and most of the subsequent ones have talked about.

By the late 1980s, program-based evaluation was becoming a popular idea. Although not many examples of theory-based evaluation were yet published, the ideas were becoming increasingly visible. Leonard Bickman edited two issues of New Directions for Program Evaluation (1987 and 1990) that elaborated and advocated the strategy, and Lee Sechrest and A. G. Scott edited one in 1993. Lipsey wrote several articles, one explicating four different versions of program theory. Several articles addressed the subject of how to analyze data that followed the underlying assumptions of a program through time (Judd and Kenny 1981; Smith 1990; Marquart 1990; Trochim 1985). Dozens of papers appeared.

At the same time, other writers were writing about logic models. Logic models seem to be similar to program theories; at least they are if the word *theory* does not overwhelm us. If we take the word *theory* to mean the professional logic that underlies a program, then the two concepts appear to be much the same.

I wrote a paper on theory-based evaluation in 1995, published in what I thought would be an obscure book, that has received considerable attention (Weiss, 1995). The idea of basing evaluation on programs' theories of change in community-based programs received a warm welcome among evaluators and sponsors of these kinds of programs. One reason seems to be that it promised (or at least hinted at a promise) that theory-based evaluation could strengthen the validity of evaluations when random assignment is impossible, as it is in place-based programming. If the evaluation can show the series of micro-steps that lead from inputs to outcomes, then causal attribution *for all practical purposes* seems to be within reach. Although such an evaluation cannot rule out all the threats to validity we have come to know and love, it has the advantage (if things go well) of showing what processes lead to the outcomes observed; if some of the posited steps are not borne out by the data, then the study can show where the expected sequence of steps breaks down.

The Present

If the past was a period when people developed and elaborated the idea of theory-based evaluation, the present is a time when evaluators are putting the ideas into practice. A graduate student, Jo Birckmayer, and I have done a search for theory-based evaluations in the periodical literature. Mark Lipsey sent me abstracts of studies that his staff coded as "integrated theory" in the evaluation data base he collected some years ago. We are still collecting cases, and I will welcome your papers and articles. We have now inspected about thirty studies that have at least a modicum of theory orientation. This preliminary inspection has given rise to some tentative ideas.

First, quite a number of articles claim that the *programs* are theory-based, and depending on how forgiving our definition of *theory* is, many of them do seem to have a set of coherent ideas providing the basis for intervention. But many of the evaluations do not follow through on that theory; they do not collect data on crucial theoretical constructs. For example, Gottfredson (1987) reports the evaluation of a program to reduce school disorder that is reportedly based on organization development principles. However, the evaluation as published does not look at the organizational development aspects. Similarly, Campbell and Ramey (1995) evaluate an early childhood intervention program that is based on theories about enhancement of early cognitive development and the ensuing development of academic confidence, motivation, and success. The evaluation does not track the steps of the program theory.

But a number of evaluations trace the emergence of the stages posited in theory. A few of the theories are simple, what Lipsey and Pollard (1989) would probably call "one-step" theories. Sheard, Marini, Bridges, and Wagner (1976) report on lithium given to aggressive prisoners in a medium-security institution. The evaluation examined the number of violent infractions that they committed. The evaluation thus tested the theory that lithium would reduce violence. The mechanism in this case is the physiological effects that lithium produces in the body. (Actually, the theory is not simple. But the physiological element, the action of lithium in the body, has been investigated by biomedical researchers and need not form part of the evaluation.)

But some are more complex theories, and the evaluations make valiant efforts to follow them along their course. Cohen and Rice (1995) trace the effects of involving parents in prevention of adolescent substance abuse prevention. They find that parents were difficult to engage, and even when parents attended the program, they did not believe that their children's friends used drugs and so did not monitor their friendships.

Much of the work in theory-based evaluation is going on in the fields of health promotion and risk prevention. Evaluators are using theory-based approaches in programs to reduce smoking, stress, risky sexual behavior, drug abuse, adolescent pregnancy, and similar ills (for example, see Goodman and others, 1996). We have also located a few theory-based studies in mental health and health care (for example, see Bickman 1983).

Another interesting thing is that evaluators abroad are embracing the approach. When I posted a request for examples of theory-based evaluation on the listserver EVALTALK, I received papers from Rush and Ogborne (1991), in Canada; Torvatn (1995), in Norway; Kelly and Maloney (1992), in Scotland; and Milne (1995), in Australia.

Conditions Conducive to Theory-Based Evaluation. When evaluators adopt a theory-based approach, it is often for one of two reasons. The first is that the evaluator is also the program developer. A program designer, usually an academic, is engaged in a cycle of program development to deal with a particular problem. He or she develops theory, operationalizes the theory in a set of program activities, tests the program and therefore the underlying theory through evaluation, and revises the intervention. Such a cycle has a long and honorable history in several fields of what I would call applied social psychology. Evaluation is part of the ongoing series of activities by which the intervention takes shape. When the work is not that of a single individual but part of the work of an academic center devoted to the design of interventions, evaluation becomes a key feature of both theory development and program modification.

A good example is the work of Sandler and others (1992) at the Program for Prevention Research at Arizona State University who iteratively developed a family bereavement program for youngsters who had lost a parent. Based on prior research and pilot testing, the program aimed to influence four "mediators," hypothesized as implicated in child symptomatology: parental demoralization, parental warmth, discussion of grief, and stable positive events. The evaluation then collected data on the extent to which the program was associated with changes in the four mediators, and went on to study the child's psychosocial symptomatology.

Another condition that promotes a theory-based approach to evaluation is conscientious theory-based development of the program. Health promotion and risk prevention are fields where program planning is well developed: designers tend to spell out their theoretical assumptions in thoughtful detail and build programs on that foundation. Therefore it becomes easy for the evaluator to follow the tracks of theory in the evaluation. Some of the theories are relatively traditional and well established, such as social learning theory. A health promotion program provides knowledge (for example, about methods to break the smoking habit), which leads to a change in motivation and intention (willingness to try to reduce smoking), which leads to a change in practice (cessation of smoking). The change in practice is assumed to lead to the ultimate outcome, which may be reduction in cardiovascular disease. In addition, social-reinforcement theory may call for provision of social supports to encourage and sustain smoking cessation.

Social-cognitive theories of several kinds are prevalent in risk prevention. The operative mechanisms are expected to be change in knowledge, change in attitude, increase in feelings of self-efficacy, higher motivation, mastery of skills, and heightened sense of responsibility, which lead to intentions to change behavior and so on to the desired outcomes. Evaluations follow the anticipated sequence of changes over time.

Program Theory and Implementation Theory. While the subject of theory-based evaluation has been gaining adherents and attention, it has also gained confusion. As is frequently the case with an emerging idea, people have attached their own understandings to the same words. Therefore we have different varieties of recommended evaluation strategies all sailing under the flag of "theory-based evaluation." Figures 3.2–3.5 are diagrams that evaluators have used to explain how their studies have been guided by theory. The diagrams differ in level of specificity, complexity, and type of pictorial display. They also incorporate two different elements of theory, what I will call implementation theory and programmatic theory.

Figure 3.2. Theory of an Antismoking Program

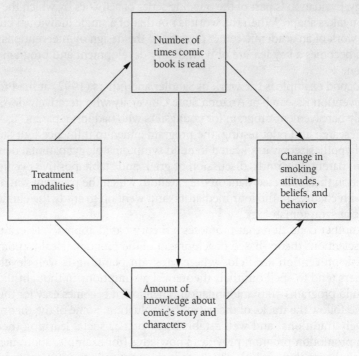

Source: Chen, Quane, Garland, and Marcin, 1988.

Implementation theory focuses on how the program is carried out. The theoretical assumption it tests is that if the program is conducted as planned, with sufficient quality, intensity, and fidelity to plan, the desired results will be forthcoming. The emphasis is on what Suchman would have called implementation failure/success. Programmatic theory, on the other hand, deals with the *mechanisms* that intervene between the delivery of program service and the occurrence of outcomes of interest. It focuses on participants' responses to program service. The mechanism of change is not the program activities per se but the response that the activities generate. For example, in a contraceptive counseling program, if counseling is associated with reduction in pregnancy, the cause of change might seem to be the counseling. But the mechanism is not the counseling; that is the program activity, the program process. The mechanism might be the knowledge that participants gain from the counseling. Or it might be that the existence of the counseling program helps to overcome cultural taboos against family planning; it might give women confidence and bolster their assertiveness in sexual relationships; it might trigger a shift in the power relations between men and women. These or any of several other cognitive, affective, social responses could be the mechanisms leading to desired outcomes.

Figure 3.3. Community Prevention Model for Alcohol and Other Drug Abuse

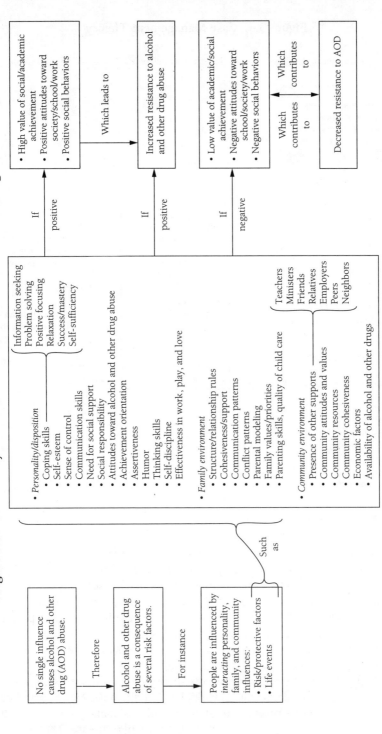

Source: Goodman and Wandersman, 1994, p. 10.

This is a working model. There are other factors, such as genetics.

Figure 3.4. Case Management Theory

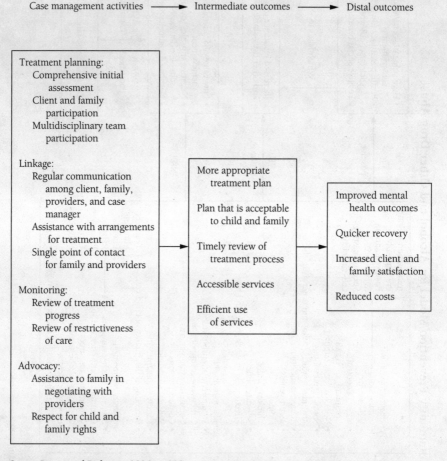

Case management activities ⟶ Intermediate outcomes ⟶ Distal outcomes

Treatment planning:
    Comprehensive initial
        assessment
    Client and family
        participation
    Multidisciplinary team
        participation

Linkage:
    Regular communication
        among client, family,
        providers, and case
        manager
    Assistance with arrangements
        for treatment
    Single point of contact
        for family and providers

Monitoring:
    Review of treatment
        progress
    Review of restrictiveness
        of care

Advocacy:
    Assistance to family in
        negotiating with
        providers
    Respect for child and
        family rights

More appropriate
    treatment plan

Plan that is acceptable
    to child and family

Timely review of
    treatment process

Accessible services

Efficient use
    of services

Improved mental
    health outcomes

Quicker recovery

Increased client and
    family satisfaction

Reduced costs

Source: Bryant and Bickman, 1996, p. 123.

Similarly, programs that aim to teach students understanding of other cultures may assume that any good results observed are due to the teaching. But teaching is not the mechanism. The mechanism is what students get from the teaching—knowledge or heightened interest, motivation, even anxiety. An evaluation that attempts to track the theoretical underpinnings of the program has to devise ways to define and measure the psychosocial, physiological, economic, sociological, organizational, or other processes that intervene between exposure to the program and participant outcomes.

Much evaluation that is purportedly theory-based actually examines outcomes in terms of implementation variables. For example, McGraw and others (1996) evaluated a program to change students' dietary knowledge and food choices so as to reduce the risk of cardiovascular disease. The program,

Figure 3.5. Program Theory of an Employment Training Program

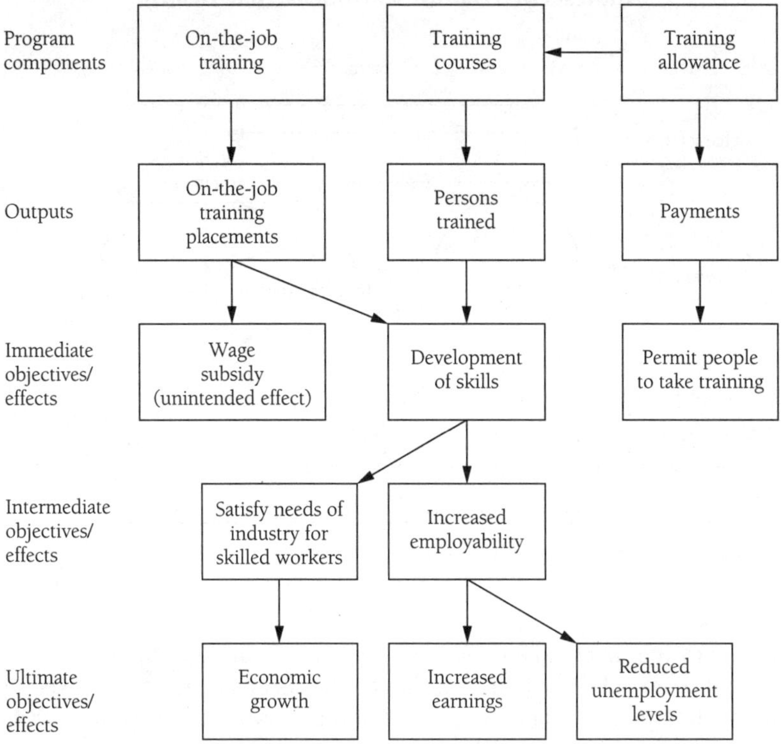

Source: Auditor General of Canada, 1981, p. 14.

called CATCH (Child and Adolescent Trial for Cardiovascular Health), had several components, but the part recently reported related to the classroom component. The outcomes studied were the children's dietary knowledge, self-confidence that they could select better foods, and intentions to eat more wisely. See Figure 3.6. These were analyzed against input variables (mainly student and teacher characteristics) and program processes, such as the extent to which teachers completed the full course of CATCH classroom activities ("dose") and the degree to which teachers modified the activities ("fidelity" to plan). The analysis led to conclusions about the extent to which program activities as defined by CATCH planners led to desired health knowledge and intended behaviors.

This study makes excellent use of process measures in analyzing outcomes. But it does not provide a test of the programmatic theory of the program, at least in this paper. The theory underlying the program is described as "modification of psychosocial factors . . . lead[ing] to changes in risk-factor behaviors" (McGraw and others, 1996, p. 292). The evaluation reported does not address the modification of psychosocial factors—that is, it does not

Figure 3.6. Program Theory Model of the Child and
Adolescent Trial for Cardiovascular Health

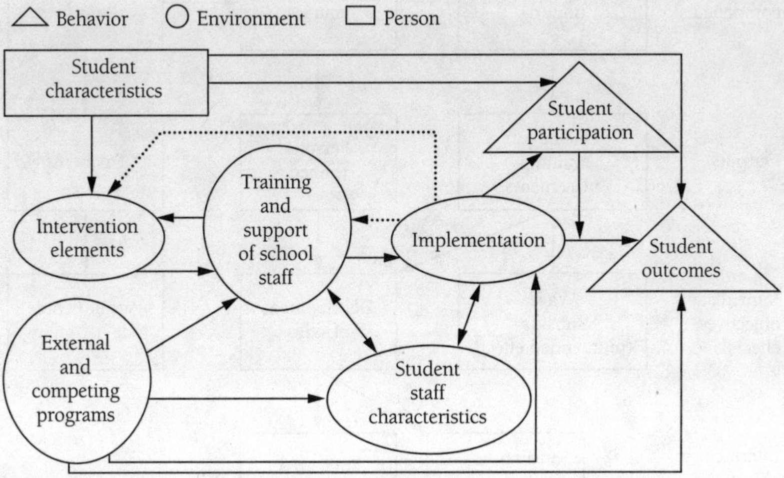

△ Behavior   ○ Environment   □ Person

Student
characteristics

Student
participation

Intervention
elements

Training
and
support
of school
staff

Implementation

Student
outcomes

External
and
competing
programs

Student
staff
characteristics

Source: McGraw and others, 1996, p. 294.

inquire into the mechanisms by which change is brought about. Similarly, Pentz and others (1990) do an excellent analysis of the relation between the implementation of a drug abuse prevention program and outcomes for adolescents. The emphasis is strictly on the extent to which implementation variables (such as exposure, adherence, fidelity, and amount of implementation) were associated with outcomes.

The difference between program theory and implementation theory is analogous to the distinction between mediator and moderator variables (Baron and Kenny, 1986). Mediator and moderator variables are both third variables that affect the relation between an independent and a dependent variable. The moderator variable is a characteristic, such as gender or frequency of exposure, the subcategories of which have different associations with the outcome variable. Girls do better than boys, or those who attend the program regularly do better than those who attend infrequently. On the other hand, a mediator variable "represents the generative mechanism through which the focal independent variable is able to influence the dependent variable of interest" (Baron and Kenny, 1986, p. 1173). That is, the moderator helps to explain which features of persons or situations have the stongest relationship to the outcome; mediators help to explain how the process works. The concepts are similar to the concepts of implementation theory and programmatic theory.

In most programs both kinds of theories will be implicated. Elsewhere I have used the term *theories of change evaluation* for evaluations that explore both elements.

The Future

Theory-based evaluation is demonstrating its capacity to help readers understand how and why a program works or fails to work. Knowing only outcomes, even if we know them with irreproachable validity, does not tell us enough to inform program improvement or policy revision. Evaluation needs to get inside the black box and to do so systematically.

One of the side benefits of this kind of evaluation is its contribution to wiser program planning even before the evaluation gets under way. When evaluators are involved in the planning phase, they have the opportunity to elicit program designers' own theories about how the program is expected to work. They can help designers to disaggregate the assumptions into the mini-steps that are implied and to confront the leaps of faith and questionable reasoning that are often involved. Evaluators can also offer theories and promising hypotheses based in the social sciences and evidence from prior evaluations that show which kinds of theories hold up in practice. In all these ways, evaluators can become profitably engaged in helping to plan programs that are rooted in better conceived premises.

Challenges lie ahead. One of the immediate needs is for better measures. Through repeated tests, evaluators have made great strides in developing valid measures of outcomes. But measurement of mediating variables is a relatively recent activity in most academic subfields, and evaluators will have to learn how to do it better. Given the large number of variables that are implied in many theories of change, measurement error makes it difficult to identify significant associations among variables—even when they are present. The field needs advances in measurement of mediating mechanisms.

Probably the central need is for better program theories. Evaluators are currently making do with the assumptions that they are able to elicit from program planners and practitioners or with the logical reasoning that they bring to the table. Many of these theories are elementary, simplistic, partial, or even outright wrong. Evaluators need to look to the social sciences, including social psychology, economics, and organization studies, for clues to more valid formulations, and they have to become better versed in theory development themselves. Better theories are important to evaluators as the backbone for their studies. Better theories are even more essential for program designers, so that social interventions have a greater likelihood of achieving the kind of society we hope for in the twenty-first century.

Theory-based evaluation can pursue two different strands in the coming years. One path is to build more detailed program theories, so that evaluations can trace micro-steps of process all along the pathways that lead to program effects. This is like the theory of the teacher home visiting program in Figure 3.1. Each program activity and each participant response is followed along the hypothesized chain of events. There is real promise in this direction, if we iteratively test the linkages between steps and substantially improve our knowledge of how processes work. This kind of evaluation will have much to tell program funders, managers, and practitioners about what works and what does not work under a range of different conditions.

The other path that theory-based evaluation can pursue is to limit the theory to the one or two central assumptions embedded in each program. They should be premises that are significant for program success, common across a range of programs, and particularly problematic. For example, many interventions are now based on the assumption that empowering residents of low-income neighborhoods to help plan social, economic, and educational programs for their community will improve the nature of services. A central premise of these kinds of programs is that residents of the community will plan and allocate resources in ways that are more responsive to need than the professional systems of the past.

Or consider programs to make major alterations in teachers' behavior through staff development programs. The assumption here is that short-term training will be able to modify teaching patterns developed over years of education and professional practice. Another example would be efforts to change such behaviors as low school grades, delinquency, and domestic violence through programs that seek to raise self-esteem and self-confidence. Theory-based evaluation could be directed at investigating the viability of such central theoretical premises.

Evaluations that test such macro-theoretical assumptions will require multiple cases and will be difficult to do. The quest will probably be more appropriate for meta-analysis than for single studies (Cook and others, 1992). Furthermore, they will not hold much interest for funders or practitioners who are wedded to the premise being scrutinized. Professionals who run short-term staff development programs for teachers are not going to be receptive to studies that question whether staff development is a sensible approach to changing teacher behavior.

Still there are audiences who want to know. Program sponsors and funders, whether foundations or government agencies, should have an intense interest in whether the strategy in which they are investing is feasible across a range of conditions. A meta-analysis of evaluations that have measured and examined the same central assumption should have important news to report. It should be able to give insight into the conditions under which these hypotheses hold and the conditions under which they result in shortfalls of varying dimensions. My long-range hope is that evaluation will not only be based on theory but also *contribute* to the cumulation of theoretical knowledge.

Conclusion

Looking at conditions of program implementation that are associated with better outcomes is a real contribution to the improvement of programs. These process/outcome evaluations show which program processes yield positive benefits. Evaluations will provide even more valuable information when they address the mechanisms that mediate between processes and outcomes. Theory-based evaluations attend not only to what programs do but also to how participants respond. Such evaluations are not easy to do, but there are circumstances in which evaluators should proceed in that direction. As a starting point, we need plausible theories. We need to make the maximum use of logical reasoning, practitioner wisdom, prior evaluations, and social science research to generate program theories and then use our collective evaluation work to test them under realistic operating conditions.

References

Auditor General of Canada. *Audit Guide: Auditing of Procedures for Effectiveness.* Ottawa: Office of Auditor General, 1981.

Baron, R. M., and Kenny, D. A. "The Moderator-Mediator Variable Distinction in Social Psychological Research: Conceptual, Strategic, and Statistical Considerations." *Journal of Personality and Social Psychology,* 1986, *51* (6), 1173–1182.

Bickman, L. "The Evaluation of Prevention Programs." *Journal of Social Issues,* 1983, *39* (1), 181–194.

Bickman, L. (ed.). *Using Program Theory in Evaluation.* New Directions for Program Evaluation, no. 33. San Francisco: Jossey-Bass, 1987.

Bickman, L. (ed.). *Advances in Program Theory.* New Directions for Program Evaluation, no. 47. San Francisco: Jossey-Bass, 1990.

Bryant, D. M., and Bickman, L. "Methodology for Evaluating Mental Health Case Management." *Evaluation and Program Planning,* 1996, *19,* 5–16.

Campbell, F. A., and Ramey, C. T. "Cognitive and School Outcomes for High-Risk African-American Students at Middle Adolescence: Positive Effects of Early Intervention." *American Educational Research,* 1995, *32* (4), 743–772.

Chen, H.-T. *Theory-Driven Evaluation: A Comprehensive Perspective.* Newbury Park, Calif.: Sage, 1990.

Chen, H.-T. "Theory-Driven Evaluations: Needs, Difficulties, and Options." *Evaluation Practice,* 1994, *15,* 79–82.

Chen, H.-T., Quane, J., Garland, T. N., and Marcin, P. "Evaluating an Antismoking Program: Diagnostics of Underlying Causal Mechanisms." *Evaluation and the Health Professions,* 1988, *11* (4), 441–464.

Chen, H.-T., and Rossi, P. H. "The Multi-Goal, Theory-Driven Approach to Evaluation: A Model Linking Basic and Applied Social Science." *Social Forces,* 1980, *59,* 106–122.

Chen, H.-T., and Rossi, P. H. "Evaluating with Sense: The Theory-Driven Approach." *Evaluation Review,* 1983, *7,* 283–302.

Chen, H.-T., and Rossi, P. H. "The Theory-Driven Approach to Validity." *Evaluation and Program Planning,* 1987, *10,* 95–103.

Cohen, D. A., and Rice, J. C. "A Parent-Targeted Intervention for Adolescent Substance Use Prevention: Lessons Learned." *Evaluation Review,* 1995, *19* (2), 159–180.

Cook, T. D., Cooper, H., Cordray, D. S., Hartmann, H., Hedges, L. V., Light, R. J., Louis, T. A., and Mosteller, F. *Meta-Analysis for Explanation: A Casebook.* New York: Russell Sage Foundation, 1992.

Fitz-Gibbon, C. T., and Morris, L. L. "Theory-Based Evaluation." *Evaluation Comment,* 1975, *5* (1), 1–4.

Goodman, R. M., and Wandersman, A. "FORECAST: A Formative Approach to Evaluating Community Coalitions and Community-Based Initiatives." *American Journal of Community Psychology,* 1994, special issue, 6–25.

Goodman, R. M., Wandersman, A., Chinman, M., Imm, P., and Morrissey, E. "An Ecological Assessment of Community-Based Interventions for Prevention and Health Promotion: Approaches to Measuring Community Coalitions." *American Journal of Community Psychology,* 1996.

Gottfredson, D. C. "An Evaluation of an Organization Development Approach to Reducing School Disorder." *Evaluation Review,* 1997, *11* (6), 739–763.

Judd, C. M., and Kenny, D. A. "Process Analysis: Estimating Mediation in Treatment Evaluations." *Evaluation Review,* 1981, *5* (5), 602–619.

Kelly, M. P., and Maloney, W. A. "A Behavioural Modelling Approach to Curriculum Development and Evaluation of Health Promotion for Nurses." *Journal of Advanced Nursing,* 1992, *17,* 544–547.

Lipsey, M. W., and Pollard, J. A. "Driving Toward Theory in Program Evaluation: More Models to Choose From." *Evaluation and Program Planning,* 1989, *12,* 317–328.

Marquart, J. M., "A Pattern-Matching Approach to Link Program Theory and Evaluation Data." In L. Bickman (ed.), *Advances in Program Theory.* New Directions for Program Evaluation, no. 47. San Francisco: Jossey-Bass, 1990.

McGraw, S. A., Sellers, D. E., Stone, E. J., Bebchuk, J., Edmundson, E. W., Johnson, C. C., Bachman, K. J., and Luepker, R. V. "Using Process Data to Explain Outcomes: An Illustration from the Child and Adolescent Trial for Cardiovascular Health (CATCH)." *Evaluation Review,* 1996, *20* (3), 291–312.

Milne, C. "Using Program Logic as a Practical Evaluation Tool: Case Studies from an Australian Evaluator." Paper given at First International Evaluation Conference, Vancouver, 1995.

Pentz, M. A., Trebow, E. A., Hansen, W. B., MacKinnon, D. P., Dwyer, J. H., Johnson, C. A., Flay, B. R., Daniels, S., and Cormack, C. "Effects of Program Implementation on Adolescent Drug Use: The Midwestern Prevention Project (MPP)." *Evaluation Review,* 1990, *14* (3), 264–289.

Quane, J. "Back from the Future: Can Evaluation Survive Dissension in the Ranks." Paper prepared for American Evaluation Association meeting, Boston, Nov. 1994.

Rush, B., and Ogborne, A. "Program Logic Models: Expanding Their Role and Structure for Program Planning and Evaluation." *Canadian Journal of Program Evaluation,* 1991, *6* (2), 95–106.

Sandler, I. N., West, S. G., Baca, L., Pillow, D. R., Gersten, J. C., Rogosch, F., Virdin, L., Beals, J., Reynolds, K. D., Kallgren, C., Tein, J-Y., Kriege, G., Cole, E., and Ramirez, R. "Linking Empirically Based Theory and Evaluation: The Family Bereavement Program." *American Journal of Community Psychology,* 1992, *20* (4), 491–521.

Sechrest, L. B., and Scott, A. G. (eds.). *Understanding Causes and Generalizing About Them.* New Directions for Program Evaluation, no. 57. San Francisco: Jossey-Bass, 1993.

Sheard, M. H., Marini, J. L., Bridges, C. L., and Wagner, E. "The Effect of Lithium on Impulsive Aggressive Behavior in Man." *American Journal of Psychiatry,* 1976, *133* (12), 1409–1413.

Smith, N. L. "Using Path Analysis to Develop and Evaluate Program Theory." In L. Bickman (ed.), *Advances in Program Theory.* New Directions for Program Evaluation, no. 47. San Francisco: Jossey-Bass, 1990.

Suchman, E. *Evaluative Research.* New York: Russell Sage Foundation, 1967.

Torvatn, H. "Chains of Reasoning: An Evaluation Tool." Trondheim, Norway: SINTEF-IFTM paper, 1995.

Trochim, W.M.K. "Pattern Matching, Validity, and Conceptualization in Program Evaluation." *Evaluation Review,* 1985, *9,* 575–604.

Weiss, C. H. *Evaluation Research: Methods for Assessing Program Effectiveness.* Englewood Cliffs N.J.: Prentice Hall, 1972.

Weiss, C. H. "Nothing as Practical as Good Theory." In J. Connell, A. Kubisch, L. B. Schorr, and C. H. Weiss (eds.), *New Approaches to Evaluating Community Initiatives.* New York: Aspen Institute, 1995.

Wholey, J. S. *Evaluation: Promise and Performance.* Washington, D.C.: Urban Institute, 1979.
Wholey, J. S. *Evaluation and Effective Public Management.* Boston: Little, Brown, 1983.
Worthen, B. "Editor's Note: The Origins of Theory-Based Evaluation." *Evaluation Practice,* 1996, *17* (2), 169–171.

CAROL H. WEISS is professor of education at the Harvard Graduate School of Education.

Advances in quantitative methods enable evaluators to collect and analyze data more efficiently, more cost-effectively, and with greater precision and sensitivity.

Advances in Quantitative Evaluation, 1987–1996

Peter H. Rossi

Many of the advances that take hold in a given decade may not have originated in that period. It takes some time for an innovation to become established. Advances in quantitative evaluation practices are no exception. Accordingly, the topic of this chapter is defined as the advances that became widely used by quantitatively inclined evaluators in the decade 1987–1996. Many of the advances discussed actually originated earlier.

I have also divided the advances into three types: facilitating advances, consisting of changes that made the carrying out of quantitative evaluation easier; advances in measurement; and advances in statistical analysis.

Facilitating Advances

The advances classified as facilitating are ones that literally help us do our work as evaluators although they are not specific to that activity.

The End of the Tyrannies of Mainframe Computing and Secretaries. Although the development of desktop and workstation computing antedate 1987, the changes that have taken place in the past decade are truly revolutionary. In 1987, I worked on an IBM-PC XT with a ten-megabyte hard disk and a five-hundred-kilobyte memory. To make runs on my datasets meant dialing up the mainframe via a modem and waiting patiently while SPSS ground away on the mainframe. Big datasets, such as those containing census tract summaries, called for mounting multiple tapes on the mainframe and getting results, with good fortune, twenty-four hours later. And, if an error was made in the batch commands, another twenty-four hours was added on.

The 1990 census tract data are available on a CD-ROM, which I can load to my Pentium equipped with a three-gigbyte hard disk and sixty-four megabytes of RAM to get my runs in seconds, at worst. A specification error can be corrected in minutes. Best of all, my present machine cost less in constant dollars than the XT machine. Great statistical packages—SPSS, SAS, STATA, SYSTAT and so on—are available that each cost less to purchase than my average monthly bills on the old mainframe. Most packages contain statistical procedures that are much more sophisticated than anything that was available on the mainframe.

The tyranny of the mainframe is over! We are now free of dependency on it and the arrogant mandarins that ran the computing centers.

I should also mention the great graphics programs that are now on the market. Attend any professional meeting, especially in the hard sciences, and you will see slides and overheads that are breathtakingly beautiful. Programs are now available that can make it possible for each of us to communicate more effectively using graphics.

The desktop and workstation computers—the distinction between them is now blurred—also liberate us from the tyranny of secretaries and typists. I have typed and edited my stuff using WordPerfect since 1985. The smell of rubber cement and correction fluid no longer hangs over my desk. I believe we now can write more and write better than before. And we do not have to wait in line to get it typed up.

Of course, there is a downside to the desktop and workstation revolution. More powerful tools are also accessible to the poorly trained and statistically challenged than ever before. I venture that there are more mindless factor analyses run in the past decade than ever before.

Data Collection. Closely related to the computing revolution are remarkable advances in data collection. A decade or so ago, the collection of survey data on more than a local basis was almost exclusively the prerogative of the few big academic survey centers and the big commercial firms that had national networks of interviewers. In the past decade, random digit dialing (RDD) and its variants have democratized data collection. It does not take much capital to set up a telephone survey center: the result is that there must be hundreds of university survey centers and undoubtedly magnitudes many more small firms that have that capability. Using RDD approaches and a small cadre of interviewers, these small survey centers can conduct nationwide telephone surveys. In addition, computer-assisted telephone interviewing systems (CATI) have made it possible for everyone to collect survey data in a highly controlled, standardized way.

Although the combination of RDD and CATI seemed initially to promise a reduction in the costs of data collection, the savings were not as large as anticipated. An RDD survey is typically only 10 to 20 percent cheaper than a face-to-face survey of comparable quality, far from the anticipated cost reductions of 50 percent or more. The emphasis in the last sentence should be placed on "comparable quality." Obtaining a high response rate on an RDD survey drives cost up considerably. Of course, even when of very high quality, an RDD survey is still restricted to telephone households. Populations often of special interest to evaluators—low-income, disadvantaged subgroups, such as the homeless—are difficult to reach by phone when they have phones and often do not have them.

On balance, the development and fine tuning of RDD and CATI survey procedures in the past decade have helped evaluators (and others) to do more survey work with some cost savings. Especially important is that these developments have widely spread the capacity for conducting large-scale surveys, with the potential of reducing inequality among evaluators.

Public-Use Datasets. Related to data collection has been the establishment in the past decade of norms calling for open access to datasets. The datasets available through data archives, notably the Inter-University Consortium on Political and Social Research, make it possible for all of us to have datasets that in the past only the most fortunate grantspersons could ever expect to collect. Datasets costing millions—such as the Public Use Census datasets, the Survey of Income and Program Participation, High School and Beyond, the National Health Survey, and the American Housing Survey—are all available. If you are in a university that belongs to the consortium, all you need is a modem, and any of the hundreds of excellent datasets can be downloaded to your hard disk in a matter of minutes. Commercial firms are also in the dataset distribution business: Sociometrics, for example, will sell you the datasets from scores of evaluation studies.

The main advance here is that a norm favoring or even requiring that datasets be made accessible in a form for public use has been established. This change will raise the standards for much research. At the least, it will make for better and more relevant master's theses and doctoral dissertations.

Advances in Communication. In the past decade, advances in communications have materially and substantially enabled us to work better. Some form of electronic communication was available before. In the late 1970s my colleague Dick Berk, then at University of California at Santa Barbara, and I carried out a cross-continent collaboration using telephone conversations and three-hundred-baud modem connections to the mainframe computers in Amherst and Santa Barbara. At the time we marveled that it only took thirty minutes to transmit an ASCII version of a thirty-page chapter. We carried out our latest collaboration via e-mail, exchanging megabyte datasets and word processor text files at no cost, and with transmissions completed in at most a few hours. E-mail makes it possible for me to collaborate with colleagues all over the country and to be in touch with literally scores of others.

Although the greatest advantages of the revolution in communications are reaped when long distances are involved, there are also advantages for local communication as well. Many of my colleagues do their work in their home, finding e-mail a better way to keep in touch than face-to-face contact in the hallways outside their university offices.

I will not comment extensively on the World Wide Web: I think the jury is still out. My own experiences (and those of many others) with the World Wide

Web has been quite disappointing. My searches have been time-consuming and have yielded a very high proportion of dross to pay dirt. Maybe I do not know how to search efficiently, and perhaps my information needs are too picky. However, as things stand now, my judgment is that the World Wide Web is not an appreciable addition to our research capacity. But the World Wide Web is still evolving and may yet become as indispensable to our work as computerized library catalogues.

Advances in Measurement

Although I have not made an enumeration, I am certain it is a safe bet that scores of measurement devices—inventories, scales, indexes—have been constructed and have been subjected to psychometric torture over the past decade. No doubt these are advances that deserve treatment at the hands of someone who keeps up with such matters. I will simply assert here that they have been done and will move on to basic advances in measurement.

First, there have been important advances in how to deal with missing values. When I began to explore the large public-use datasets released by the Census Bureau, I first began to become aware that the reason the Census Bureau's published tables never reported any missing values was that when data were missing, the Census Bureau imputed values for the missing values. The Census Bureau did not drop cases, as I had been doing, nor did it substitute grand means, as some of my benighted colleagues did. Rather, they inserted values from the nearest similar case found in the dataset. When I got over my shock about this concealment on the part of the Census Bureau statisticians, I began to realize that their data doctoring made some sense.

In the past few years, statisticians, notably Donald Rubin (1987), have worked out and tested a set of rational procedures for the imputation of missing values and to correct the statistical inference measures for the resulting dataset. The underlying rationale of the procedures is to take advantage of the existing information about a case in which a given value is missing in order to make an informed estimate of the most likely value for missing item. For example, a common imputation for a missing value on a single item in a multi-item scale is to use as a substitute the predicted value ($\hat{Y}$) obtained from the regression of all the other items on the score for that item. This imputed value has the attractive feature of using what we know about a case. Of course, these methods work best when the substantive area involved is strongly structured and when the case for which a value is missing has enough information that is not missing.

A second advance in measurement is the use of ideas from experimental designs in collecting data. I will describe the approach I know best—because I developed it—the factorial survey method (Rossi and Nock, 1982). The main impetus for its development arose out of frustration with the limitations of surveys in dealing with complex topics. For example, survey items dealing with respondents' views of the criminal justice system typically asked overly simple questions. For two decades the General Social Survey has used the following item to get at how people assessed the working of our court system: "In general, do you think the courts in this area deal too harshly or not harshly enough with criminals?"

Over the past twenty years, about 80 percent of the American population has responded that the courts were not harsh enough. The over-simplifications should be obvious: Which courts? Local, state, or federal? Which criminals? Property crime offenders? Felons convicted of violent crimes? White-collar criminals? Those convicted of misdemeanors? What do respondents know about actual sentencing practices?

Substitute your favorite substantive area for the "courts in this area"—such as public welfare, child welfare agencies, child abuse/neglect, and so on—and the result will be quite typical survey items. All of the public issues are magnitudes more complicated than can be accommodated within single items. These overly simple questions also cannot do justice to the complexity of respondent judgments that, in the case of the courts, distinguish between the civil and criminal courts, between violent crime and white collar offenses, and so on.

Properly to gauge the beliefs and judgments of individuals on any complex topic, we need a multitude of items, a strategy that would tax the capacity of survey instruments and certainly the patience of respondents.

Melding the methodologies of randomized experiments and sample surveys, the factorial survey approach provides a solution to studying complex substantive areas. It proceeds by breaking up the complexity of some issue into as many dimensions as needed, constructing items by combining levels from each dimension into vignettes, and presenting respondents with a sample of the resulting combinations as short descriptive vignettes. For example, in a study of public views on the sentencing of criminals in the courts (Rossi and Berk, 1997), we constructed vignette descriptions of convicted felons by systematically varying the crime committed, the damage inflicted, and the gender and previous record of the depicted offender. Because the vignettes were assembled by randomly picking a level from each of the dimensions, each of the vignettes more closely approximated the complexity of actual cases. The respondents were asked to give their desired punishments to persons convicted of the crimes described in the vignettes.

Note that an important feature of this approach is that each respondent is presented with an independently drawn random sample of vignettes. In the case of the study just described, the number of possible unique vignettes numbered in the millions, but each respondent received a random sample of forty-two. However, combining the respondent samples produced a pooled sample of vignettes large enough to say something about how Americans would like to sentence various crimes, how they take previous record of criminals into account, how they would alter sentences in response to previous record or sex of the criminal, and so on.

Of course, the factorial survey approach is a general one that can be applied to many substantive areas, such as the perceived equity of welfare payments, definitions of child abuse, ethical dilemmas in medical practice, definitions of sexual harassment, perceptions of the social standing of households, or the justice of income distributions. The main issues in these studies all involve ascertaining how judgments are affected by the dimensions that make up complex social issues.

The third advance in measurement I will touch on is one that is currently under way and is beginning to affect quantitative research. Writing items for use in schedules or questionnaires has traditionally been a matter of craftlore rather than science. By craftlore, I mean practice based on the experience of recognized craftspersons. Guided by their experiences with what works, craftlore-based manuals on how to write survey questions are rich in examples but poor in stating general principles about how best to write reliable and valid items. The knowledge imparted might be valuable but tends to be highly particular, as opposed to general, and is lacking in firm scientific bases.

The advances in this decade have come from two directions. On the one hand, there has developed a tradition of experimentation with question wording, exemplified by the work of Howard Schuman and Stanley Presser (Schuman and Presser, 1996). Through their work we are beginning to understand how much responses to items are affected by question wording, the placement of items in various contexts, and other formal characteristics of items. On the other hand, building on the base of cognitive psychology, work is currently under way constructing response theory, consisting of general principles concerning how the formal characteristics of items affect responses to the items. Here the work summarized in Tanur (1992) is of special importance.

None of these attempts to put item writing on a firm theoretical and empirical foundation as yet have fully succeeded. We may be some years from the time when item writing can be taught systematically. It will not mean that we will be able to do without craftspersons, but it will mean that the road to experience will be somewhat faster and will be traveled more successfully by more persons.

Advances (and Some Retreats) in Statistical Analysis

It is difficult to separate the advances in statistical analyses from the advances in statistical computing power available to researchers. Clearly the tremendous increase in what it is possible to do with our new machines stimulates the development of statistical models to handle problems that were discerned earlier at a time when nothing could be done about them.

It is also the case that the development of new and sophisticated statistical models is a terrible temptation to the foolish and unsophisticated. I would be moderately richer if I got a modest fee for each fatally flawed article I have reviewed for scholarly journals whose failure could be reasonably interpreted as the work of someone who tried to remedy a bad study by using a sophisticated statistical model that he or she did not understand.

There are six statistical modeling advances that I have identified. I am certain that there are more than six, but that was all I was able to assemble with the combination of my recall ability and that of the nonrandom sample of quantitative evaluation experts whom I consulted. Not unexpectedly, these are techniques I know about because they are addressed to problems I have encountered.

Hierarchical Linear Modeling. This is a useful approach to nested data, such as students nested within classes, residents clustered in census tracts, patients nested within hospitals, and so on. The research problem is how to disentangle the effects of different levels of aggregation, a problem known for a long time under the rubric of the "ecological fallacy," for example. The best illustration I know of is the recent monograph by Anthony Bryk and his colleagues (Bryk, Lee, and Holland, 1993). The problem they come to grips with is how to explain why students in Catholic high schools outperform students in the public high schools on achievement tests. Are these differences school effects or compositional effects? Using hierarchical linear modeling, Bryk shows convincingly that the Catholic high schools are different primarily because the schools are differently organized—for example, there are fewer electives, so all students more or less take the same classes and are not tracked into superior and inferior curricula. Most important, the teachers and students in Catholic high schools expressed a deep sense of community and commitment to the schools.

Hierarchical linear modeling is important for evaluators. Many of the programs we attempt to evaluate generate data that have nesting characteristics. Many programs deal with neighborhoods, communities, public or private agencies, school districts, schools, work units, or other organized entities, all of which produce nested data. The statistical problem presented by such data can now be addressed by hierarchical linear models and "mixed model" forms of analysis of variance (Bryk and Raudenbush, 1992; Goldstein, 1995.)

Selection Bias Modeling. The gold standard research design for impact assessments is the randomized controlled experiment. The overwhelmingly desirable characteristic of such designs is their ability to rule out selection bias as a competing explanation for findings. Target populations who end up as participants in programs arrive there by complicated and usually unknown processes involving self-selection and administrative selection. Randomized experiments substitute random selection for the unknown selection processes and thereby produce impact estimates that are free from selection processes.

Unfortunately, as we all know, randomized controlled experiments are expensive, time-consuming, and all too often politically or ethically unacceptable. In principle, if the selection processes were known and measurable, we could use that knowledge to model selection processes and arrive at unbiased estimates using nonexperimental data. A statistical model based on that idea has been proposed by econometrician James Heckman (Heckman and Hotz, 1989). The major applications of his model have been in the evaluation of employment training programs, but there have been many attempts to use his approach in the analysis of other nonexperimental impact assessments of other programs.

The general idea behind Heckman's selection bias modeling approach is to compare program participants and nonparticipants holding selection processes constant. Like that of other modeling approaches, its utility strongly depends on how well the model is specified. Heckman and his colleagues have produced several illustrative examples of how his approach can be used to produce seemingly successful effectiveness estimates.

Used by a variety of researchers, Heckman's approach has produced contradictory results, showing great sensitivity to differences in specification. Although the jury is still out on Heckman's specific approach, the general ideas lying behind it deserve some attention. If it could be used by different researchers obtaining consistent results, the evaluation field would benefit greatly.

There is a curious Catch–22 twist to the use of Heckman's model. That model is best tested when we compare results obtained from its use with results from a randomized experiment. The catch arises because the main reason one would want to employ it is to substitute for randomization. Accordingly, the efficient use of Heckman's approach occurs when you do not have the opportunity to use a randomized approach. But the only way you can be sure that selection bias modeling works is to compare its results with those of a randomized experiment.

I think it is appropriate to mention the several important studies that have been made over the past decade comparing the results from randomized experiments with those from attempts to use nonrandomized controls. The most interesting work along these lines was done by Friedlander and Robins (1994) of the Manpower Demonstration Research Corporation. They used the datasets from four randomized experiments conducted on welfare-to-work programs in Baltimore, Arkansas, Virginia, and San Diego. The effect values from the randomized experiments were compared with those derived from nonrandomized controls. In one set of comparisons, the control groups were formed out of the randomized control groups of the other experiments. That is, the experimental group, say in San Diego, was compared with the control groups in Baltimore, Virginia, and Arkansas. In another case the control groups were formed out of the randomized control groups from other sites within the same experiment. In still another case, statistical controls were introduced in an attempt to make the comparison groups match more closely the experimental group. In all of the comparisons, the effects derived from the comparisons between the experimental groups and the "pseudo" controls were markedly different from those computed from the experiments. The effects were sometimes larger and sometimes smaller or even of opposite sign. The main point here is that it is very difficult to construct a comparison group that closely resembles in statistical properties control groups constructed by randomization.

Meta-Analyses. A dramatic development in the past decade has been the growing popularity of meta-analyses, in which the results from many studies of some given phenomenon are studied jointly in order to arrive at the central tendencies in that set of studies. Of course, literature reviews have been around for a long time, but qualitative methods are not very good at summarizing fairly large numbers of studies, tending to rest conclusions on a small selection of the often rather large pool of studies available. For example, in the 1970s a conventional literature review of criminal rehabilitation evaluations conducted by Lipton, Martinson, and Wilks (1975) came to the depressing conclusion that nothing works. I have no doubt that the authors tried hard to summarize in an even-handed fashion the literally hundreds of studies. Unfortunately, it is extremely difficult to be even-handed without having the tools at hand to discipline the selection of studies and identify the central tendencies of the studies reviewed, taking into account their quality. When two of the authors approached the task in the 1980s using meta-analytic methods, they came to much modified conclusions, indicating that there were kinds of rehabilitative programs that worked and that programs evaluated with research designs that had high internal validity tended to have stronger effects.

The essentials of the procedures employed in meta-analyses are familiar to most evaluators. There are many examples of how much we can learn from them. Nevertheless, meta-analysis does have some limitations. For example, there is the issue of publication selection. In a recent meta-analysis I read of the evaluation of sex education programs (Kirby, 1994), intended to lower the incidence of teen age pregnancy, some twenty-four program evaluations were found and used. About three of the twenty-four showed significant positive effects, and twenty-one showed positive effects that were not significant, but *none* showed negative effects. Clearly the programs as a group were ineffective, but the anomaly is that none of the studies had negative effects! I interpret this finding as possible evidence of publication bias: studies finding negative effects simply may have not been published.

Despite these (and other) problems, meta-analyses show great promise. Perhaps the most important contribution of this approach is its ability to extract some sense from the welter of evaluation studies that have accumulated over the past few decades. A great deal of work has been done, which uncollected and unsummarized leads to a sense of inconsistency and confusion. Meta-analysis extends the promise of making sense out of that seeming chaos.

Advances in the Statistical Analysis of Categorical Data. Many of the critical outcome measures in which evaluation researchers are interested are intrinsically categorical: for example, in child welfare evaluations preventive programs may be concerned with lowering the probabilities that children at risk are abused, neglected, or both. Or a welfare-to-work program evaluation may be concerned with raising the probability of an AFDC client becoming employed. A program working with the homeless may be concerned with raising the probability of shelter residents becoming housed. As we all know, such categorical outcome variables have distributional characteristics that do not easily fit the requirements for ordinary least squares and other models designed for continuous variables. In addition, many of the designs used lead to censored observations. For example, we may be able to follow homeless shelter clients for six months after program participation with the result that we cannot observe outcomes beyond that period.

Statistical models that are based on the special distributional characteristics of categorical data have been around for a long time. What makes this decade different from previous periods is that knowledge about them has diffused from the biostatistics field, where they mainly originated, to social research. The migration has been mightily aided by the growing power of the personal computers and workstations in use in our field. All the major statistics packages—SAS, SPSS, STATA—now contain procedures for handling a variety of such models. The statistics package I use, STATA, has more than a dozen procedures including robust versions.

Logistic regression and its variants, including probit, hazard models, ordered logit, and so on, have come to be used routinely in our field in the past decade. I believe that this diffusion has enriched the abilities of evaluation research to produce credible research.

Of course, there is a downside to this development. After much work I believe we have educated our audiences sufficiently that they now can understand the results of OLS regressions and ANOVA. R^2, or standardized and unstandardized regression coefficients, is now entering the common discourse in the courts and policy circles. Odds ratios and relative risk measures are not as easily understandable by those outside the evaluation fraternity, and often have a hard time within it. I have had considerable difficulty explaining the relative risk measures resulting from an ordered logit analysis of the outcomes of child abuse investigations to an audience of child welfare officials. Indeed, I do not think I succeeded, although I am sure that I wore them down.

Statistical Inference from Complex Multistage Samples. I believe that the most important advance in applied social research in the last half of the twentieth century was the development of practical methods for the probability sampling of human populations. Major public use datasets on which we all rely—such as the Current Population Survey, the General Social Survey, and the Survey of Income and Program Participation—are all based on multistage area probability samples. The basic sampling strategy in such surveys consists of selection stages in which the first is the selection of relatively large areas—counties, metropolitan statistical areas—with probabilities proportionate to size, then sampling smaller areas, such as tracts or enumeration districts, and then sampling blocks within the selected tracts, and then finally selecting households within blocks. Even random digit dialing surveys are often multistage samples in which area codes are selected in the first stage, telephone business offices in the second stage, and individual telephone numbers in the final stage.

The advantage of multistage sampling strategies are obvious. For face-to-face interview data collection, the cost advantage of the resulting clustering in space of households selected in the last stage results in highly cost-effective data collection, reducing travel and interviewing time to reach the selected households. The downside is that the resulting samples are not the equivalent of random samples, although they are unbiased samples. The undesirable feature resulting from the clustering in space of selected households is that the resulting observations are not independent. That is, there is some degree of within-cluster correlation resulting from the fact that the residents of a given small area tend to resemble each other more than they resemble residents of other areas. Even more disturbing is that the degree of intra-cluster correlation varies by kind of measurement. For example, the intra-cluster correlation is likely to be higher for measures related closely to income than for measures related closely to gender. As we all know, the intra-cluster correlation results from the fact of residential segregation by socioeconomic status, race, ethnicity, and age. The intra-cluster correlations are not very high, but they are high enough to lower the power of a survey of a given size appreciably relative to the power of a simple random sample of equivalent size. In other words, standard errors correctly computed on measures obtained from a multistage clustered sample are nearly always larger than those computed from a simple random sample of the same size.

What all this means is that handling a multistage clustered sample as if it were a simple random sample is almost always incorrect. The measures are unbiased, but the standard errors are incorrect and understated. In many cases, especially when the sample sizes are very large, it may not matter that such standard errors are incorrect because if they were corrected it would not make much difference. If your incorrectly computed t statistic was 45.5, the corrected value was likely more than 20, meaning that either way the measure was highly significant.

Up to the current decade, almost all researchers using data from multistage surveys ignored the issue. This was a dirty little secret we all shared in common. However, we all had a very good excuse: there was no practical way to compute the correct standard errors. Analytical models existed, but their computational forms were too complicated and clumsy to use. The important advance in the current period is the development of brute-force practical methods for the computation of more nearly correct inference measures. Bootstrap and jackknife computational approaches plus the increased available computational capacity are making it no longer necessary to practice statistical hypocrisy. The new approaches essentially estimate the sampling errors empirically by repeated sampling (with replacement) from the sample observations sufficiently to arrive at an empirical estimate of the sampling variance. Both methods are computationally intensive. For example, using a relatively modest-sized multistage clustered sample with $N = 1,737$, it took about two hours on my 166-megahertz Pentium machine to develop bootstrap estimates of the standard errors for the coefficients in a five-variable OLS equation. Clearly this is a method suitable only for those with patience, to be used sparingly and intelligently when t statistics are on the edge of statistical significance.

Bootstrap and jackknife estimation procedures have not yet become standard practice, and some statistics packages do not contain such computational routines. But I notice more and more articles based on multistage survey datasets that use either jackknife or bootstrap methods to compute standard errors.

Summing Up

Summing up, this has been a good decade for advances in quantitative work. We have developed data collection methods that are efficient and less expensive. We are learning to measure concepts with greater sensitivity and precision. The new statistical methods allow us to handle data using statistical models that are more appropriate to our needs. Although many of the advances of this decade are based on the truly impressive increase in the computing power available to researchers, there also have been conceptual breakthroughs from which we can derive considerable advantage.

Of course, evolution and change never end. The next decade contains as much or more promise.

References

Bryk, A. S., Lee, V. E., and Holland, P. B. *Catholic Schools and the Common Good.* Cambridge, Mass.: Harvard University Press, 1993.

Bryk, A. S., and Raudenbush, S. W. *Hierarchical Linear Models.* Newbury Park, Calif.: Sage, 1992.

Friedlander, D., and Robins, P. *Estimating the Effect of Employment and Training Programs: An Assessment of Some Nonexperimental Techniques.* New York: Manpower Demonstration Research Corporation, 1994.

Goldstein, H. *Multilevel Statistical Models.* London: Edward Arnold Press, 1995.

Heckman, J., and Hotz, J. "Choosing Among Alternative Nonexperimental Methods for Estimating the Impact of Social Programs." *Journal of the American Statistical Association,* 1989, 84 (408), 862–880.

Kirby, D. *Sex Education in the Schools.* Menlo Park, Calif.: Henry J. Kaiser Foundation, 1994.

Lipton, D., Martinson, R., and Wilks, J. *The Effectiveness of Correctional Treatment: A Survey of Evaluation Studies.* New York: Praeger, 1975.

Rossi, P. H., and Berk, R. A. *Just Punishment: Sentencing Guidelines and Public Opinion Compared.* Hawthorne, N.Y.: Aldine de Gruyter, 1997.

Rossi, P. H., and Nock, S. *Measuring Social Judgments: The Factorial Survey Approach.* Beverly Hills: Sage, 1982.

Rubin, D. B. *Multiple Imputation for Non-Response in Surveys.* New York: Wiley & Sons, 1987.

Schuman, H., and Presser, S. *Questions and Answers in Attitude Surveys: Experiments on Question Form, Wording, and Context.* Newbury Park, Calif.: Sage, 1996.

Tanur, J. M. (ed.). *Questions About Questions: Inquiries into the Cognitive Bases of Surveys.* New York: Russell Sage Foundation, 1992.

PETER H. ROSSI is Stuart A. Rice Professor Emeritus in the department of sociology at the University of Massachusetts in Amherst.

Logic models are critical in helping evaluators understand the design and implementation of programs and advance the practice of case study approaches to evaluation.

Case Study Evaluations: A Decade of Progress?

Robert K. Yin

The American Evaluation Association's tenth-anniversary theme, "A Decade of Progress," was the inspiration and point of departure for the present article. Leonard Bickman invited me to reflect on the use of case studies in evaluation. In considering the use of case studies, the tenth-anniversary theme quickly became a question rather than an assertion: "Has the case study produced a decade['s worth] of progress?" This article addresses the question first by defining the case study method, then by examining the use of the case study method from a historical perspective, and finally by commenting on the progress (or lack of progress) during the past decade (roughly 1987 to 1997).

Definition of the Case Study Method

Critical to the discussion is the definition of the case study method. As will be pointed out shortly, two different types of research have been confused within the rubric of the case study method. Selecting one or the other type will yield different interpretations regarding the possible progress over the decade's time. Therefore, for the sake of discussion, the case study method may be briefly profiled as follows (Yin, 1994a, 1997).

A Three-Featured Profile. First, the method depends on the use of—and ability to integrate in converging fashion (some would say "triangulate")—information from multiple sources of evidence. The evidence may include direct observations, interviews, documents, archival files, and actual artifacts. The facts and conclusions for the case study will be built around the consistency of data from these sources, and these facts and conclusions may be expressed in both quantitative and qualitative terms.

Second, the method implicitly assumes a richness of data because a case study is intended to examine a phenomenon in its real-life context. Often, the boundary between the phenomenon and the context is not sharp, and inherent in all case studies is the potentially important influence of contextual conditions. A major investigative concomitant—usually taken for granted—is the need to collect case study data in the field, thereby collecting data about the context, although under unusual circumstances a case study can be conducted from library and secondary sources alone. A major technical concomitant is that case studies will always have more variables of interest than data points, effectively disarming most traditional statistical methods, which demand the reverse situation.

Third and last, the case study method includes research that contains single case studies as well as multiple-case studies. The process of generalizing the results of either type of case study depends on the development, testing, and replication of theoretical propositions (analytic generalization)—rather than any notions based on the selection of numeric samples and extrapolating to a population (statistical generalization). Especially helpful is the specification and testing of *rival* theories or explanations, which can even take place within a single case study; in a multiple-case study, one possible rationale for case selection is that certain cases have been included because they represent rivals.

Methods Falling Within and Outside the Profile. Profiling the case study in this manner provides a broad umbrella for different styles of case study research, including those based on differing philosophies of science. For instance, Bob Stake's recent book characterizes my case study research as "quantitative," appearing to contrast strongly with his own "qualitative" approach (Stake, 1995). However, examination of both approaches reveals similar ingredients. Although the qualitative approach gives less attention to multiple-case situations, it clearly draws on the same multiple sources of evidence and is concerned with the richness of case and context. Stake also agrees that the matter of defining the "case" requires close attention. Further, in discussing case study data collection and analysis, he devotes an entire chapter of his book to triangulation.

At the same time, the profile excludes certain methods that have sometimes been confused with case study research and evaluation. The primary exclusion is the classic ethnographic study—commonly using the participant-observer method (Jorgensen, 1989). Such a study traditionally focused on a preliterate society, resulting in evidence based mainly on observations and discussions but with little opportunity to rely on documentary or archival records. Ethnographic methods have been used in a variety of contemporary settings (Fetterman, 1989), including the study of organizations (such as Leonard-Barton, 1987). For evaluations, two advocates of the ethnographic method note that its strength is maximized where a strong clash in values permeates an organization or project (Lincoln and Guba, 1986). However, because the participant-observer is limited in the ability to cover multiple events occurring at the same time, many ethnographic studies also tend to be studies of small groups within a culture (or organization), rather than systematic coverage of the whole culture (or organization). If more than participant-observation is used in doing an evaluation, the resulting study may begin to resemble and be considered a case study. To this extent, judgments about inclusion or exclusion must, as always, appreciate the actual array of techniques being used, not just broad labels.

The Importance of the Profile as a Statement About Case Study Design. In her major historical overview of case studies in American methodological thought, Platt (1992) characterized our profile of the case study method as giving greater emphasis to case study *design* rather than *data collection*. The distinctiveness of the design, especially with the number of potentially relevant variables far exceeding the number of data points (often, only a single data point or "case"), forces investigators to use different strategies for establishing internal, external, and construct validity, compared to experimental or quasi-experimental research. Likewise, the need to pursue analytic and not statistical generalizations means that cross-case strategies must go beyond merely counting the number of cases, as if they were a sample of anything.

At the same time, the basic profile should not be construed as ignoring issues of data collection. Case study investigators must be intensely concerned with collecting data in a reliable and rigorous manner. In doing data collection, case study investigators also must struggle with the problem of divulging identities or maintaining the confidentiality and anonymity of sources and even of the case itself.

The Use of the Case Study Method from a Historical Perspective

From a historical perspective, Platt (1992) traces the practice of doing case studies back to three strands of research during the early twentieth century: the conduct of life histories, the work of the Chicago school of sociology, and casework in social work. She then shows how participant-observation emerged as a common data collection technique in doing these case studies. However, over time the data collection technique eventually became confused with the entirety of the case study method. The effect of this confusion on social science was dramatic, as traced by Platt. Prior to 1970, she found that twenty-nine out of thirty-one textbooks covered the topic of case studies, yet from 1970 to 1979, eighteen out of thirty textbooks published failed to mention case studies *at all*. Instead, these textbooks usually discussed participant-observation or other forms of "fieldwork" as alternative data collection techniques, reflecting the only coverage given to qualitative research.

In evaluation, this trend was serendipitously reinforced during the same period of time by the classic work of Campbell and Stanley (1963) in describing their variety of "quasi-experimental" designs. Their work—used for many

Use and Diversification of Case Study Tools. The elaboration of the case study method begins with a more refined understanding of the uses of case studies in evaluation. The GAO volume (U.S. Government Accounting Office, 1990, p. 9) explicitly lays out at least six different situations: illustrative, exploratory, critical instance, program implementation, program effects, and cumulative (meta-analysis of multiple-case studies done at different times). Each situation demands slightly different designs. For instance, the design for an illustrative case study may be limited to the point being illustrated, whereas the design for a program implementation or program effects case study requires extensive expression of presumed causal links. At the time of its publication, the GAO volume noted that existing reports tended to use only two of the six applications (illustrative and critical instance); that trend may have since broadened.

A second area of use and diversification has been in preparing for and documenting case study evidence. The use of *case study protocols* to organize the data collection—protocols that are far broader in scope than a simple questionnaire—is now commonly accepted as the most desired prelude to systematic data collection. The need for a case study protocol is especially great and has become frequent practice where multiple investigators are collaborating in doing multiple case studies, but are all still part of the same overall evaluation. Similarly, the understanding that case study evidence may be contained in a separate *case study database*—different from the actual final case study report—has taken greater hold. The database may take both narrative and tabular form, a key feature being that the noted information contains explicit footnotes or references to the specific source of the evidence (thereby helping to preserve the desired *chain of evidence*). Further, the database, though not edited or intended for public presentation, nevertheless needs to be available for independent inspection by other investigators.

However, during the decade, possibly the most important advance in tools has been the use of *logic models* as part of the design in doing case study evaluations (Yin, 1992; and Yin, 1993, pp. 65–68). A logic model presents the presumed causal sequence of events expressed in a series of cause-and-effect steps. Developed initially to carry out evaluability assessments (Wholey, 1979), the specification of logic models is a rewarding activity in at least two respects. First, the logic model reveals the underlying theory of a program that is being evaluated, and the specification of the model provides the guidance for the relevant data that need to be sought during the case study. Second, the process of putting a logic model together—especially when shared between program managers and evaluators working together—often yields insights that need not await the completion of an evaluation but that are immediately useful for program development.

At the same time, the proper and complete specification of logic models is still an evolving craft. Potentially worrisome is that the most common logic models still only identify different effects or stages but do not give an actual explanation of how events move from one stage to another. For instance, as shown in the upper part of Figure 5.1, the typical logic model consists of a series of boxes (stages) connected by a series of arrows (causal relations among the stages). The accompanying logical statements take the following form: "By implementing this activity (input), the program will engage the needed number of participants (output) and will eventually have the desired effect on these participants (outcome)." Left unstated is exactly how the activity will indeed engage the participants, or how the effect will arise from the act of participating. One possible shortcoming in these specifications has therefore been that too much attention has been given to the boxes in a logic model, and not enough to the connecting arrows. The lower part of Figure 5.1 therefore deliberately focuses attention on one set of arrows, and the challenge to the case study investigator is to associate substantive how and why explanations with the arrows.

Figure 5.1. Relating Partnership Actions to Prevention Outcomes

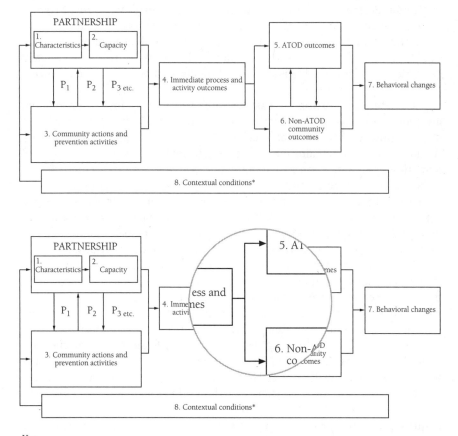

Key

P_1, P_2, P3 = Phase 1, Phase 2, Phase 3
* Other arrows from Contexual Conditions to all other components not shown

Case Study Practices During the Past Decade. Examinations of case study evaluations—and discussions with investigators attempting to do case studies—reveals greater use of these various case study tools over the decade. More important, the craft is now explicitly recognized as having tools and rigor, a norm going considerably beyond the earlier and crude notion that doing case studies mainly required an ability "to tell it like it is." With the increased availability of texts referring to and describing the case study method, investigators also have more ways of finding the needed guidance to practice the craft. Overall, the major progress in case study evaluations during the past decade may very well be the fact that investigators are knowingly pursuing practices that are part of a formal craft.

The process of doing case study evaluations also has become a more collaborative activity. Case study evaluators now work more closely with the officials of the program being evaluated to conduct the initial phases of evaluation, including the definition of the questions to be addressed by the evaluation, the evaluation design, and the preferred data collection methods. Similar trends, covered under such rubrics as "action research," "cluster evaluation," and "empowerment evaluation," are increasingly true of all evaluation methods, not just case studies. However, case study evaluations—focusing on concrete and readily understandable issues—lend themselves best to this new participatory type of evaluation.

Case Studies During the Past Decade. Whether all this documentation, awareness, and changes in practice have led to new and better kinds of case studies, however, is yet to be seen. In this sense, the final judgment on a decade of progress remains open. The routine case studies, frequently part of a multi-method evaluation design not limited to the case study method, appear to be better constructed and documented. For instance, fifteen communities were the subject of ongoing research on as contemporary a topic as managed care (Ginsburg and Fasciano, 1996). Along the same lines, graduate students, both in this country and abroad, appear to be practicing better and more rigorous case studies, especially as part of their theses or dissertations.

But the decade has not produced any particularly distinctive case studies, such as Graham Allison's *Essence of Decision* (1971), much less any landmark multiple case study evaluation. There has also not emerged any streamlined way of sharing case studies, which still require a burdensome amount of text (and hence space) that probably precludes the creation of any journal devoted to case studies (in turn limiting the amount of professional communication about case studies). Even when a study takes over the whole issue of a two-hundred-page journal ("Tracking Health System Change," 1996), as in the case of the managed care study previously cited (Ginsburg and Fasciano, 1996), the case studies are not presented as part of the publication. In these situations, a frequent problem is that the original case studies are usually too long, but there is great difficulty in preparing a second set of abbreviated texts.

At the same time, also possibly true is that the experience with case study evaluations bears great similarity to the experience with evaluation more generally (Yin, 1994b). For instance, evaluation as a whole may not have produced landmark studies during the past decade, in part because of the difficulty of improving on the exemplars of the past. Thus, interpreting the past decade of progress with case study evaluations shares the inevitable problem of interpreting many evaluation findings: no milestone stands out to any absolute extent; but somehow, conditions appear to be slightly better than before, based on process considerations—in this case, improved case study practices. Overall, and again as with the problem of interpreting many evaluation findings, possibly the passage of more time is needed to provide a more revealing, if not definitive, perspective.

References

Agranoff, R., and Radin, B. A. "The Comparative Case Study Approach in Public Administration." *Research in Public Administration,* 1991, *1,* 203–231.

Allison, G. T. *Essence of Decision: Explaining the Cuban Missile Crisis.* Boston: Little, Brown, 1971.

Benbasat, I., Goldstein, D., and Mead, M. "The Case Research Strategy in Studies of Information Systems." *MIS Quarterly,* 1987, *11,* 369–386.

Campbell, D. T. "Degrees of Freedom and the Case Study." *Comparative Political Studies,* 1975, *8,* 178–193.

Campbell, D. T., and Stanley, J. *Experimental and Quasi-Experimental Designs for Research.* Chicago: Rand McNally, 1963.

Cash, J. I., and Lawrence, P. R. (eds.). *The Information Systems Research Challenge: Qualitative Research Methods,* Vol. 1. Boston: Harvard Business School, 1989.

Cook, T. D., and Campbell, D. T. *Quasi-Experimentation: Design and Analysis Issues for Field Settings.* Chicago: Rand McNally, 1979.

Feagin, J. R., Orum, A. M., and Sjoberg, G. (eds.). *A Case for the Case Study.* Chapel Hill: University of North Carolina Press, 1991.

Fetterman, D. *Ethnography: Step by Step.* Thousand Oaks, Calif.: Sage, 1989.

Gilgun, J. F. "A Case for Case Studies in Social Work Research." *Social Work,* 1994, *39* (4), 371–380.

Ginsburg, P. B., and Fasciano, N. J. (eds.). *The Community Snapshots Project: Capturing Health System Change.* Princeton, N.J.: Robert Wood Johnson Foundation, 1996.

Jorgensen, D. *Participant Observation: A Methodology for Human Studies.* Thousand Oaks, Calif.: Sage, 1989.

Leonard-Barton, D. "Implementing Structured Software Methodologies: A Case of Innovation in Process Technology." *Interfaces,* 1987, *17,* 6–17.

Lincoln, Y. S., and Guba, E. G. *Naturalistic Inquiry.* Thousand Oaks, Calif.: Sage, 1986.

Platt, J. "'Case Study' in American Methodological Thought." *Current Sociology,* 1992, *40* (1), 17–48.

Ragin, C. C., and Becker, H. S. (eds.). *What Is a Case? Exploring the Foundations of Social Inquiry.* New York: Cambridge University Press, 1992.

Rubin, A., and Babbie, E. *Research Methods for Social Work.* (2nd ed.) Pacific Grove, Calif.: Brooks/Cole, 1993.

Stake, R. E. *The Art of Case Study Research.* Thousand Oaks, Calif.: Sage, 1995.

"Tracking Health System Change." *Health Affairs,* 1996, *15* (entire issue 2).

U.S. General Accounting Office, Program Evaluation and Methodology Division. *Case Study Evaluations.* Washington, D.C.: Government Printing Office, 1990.

Wholey, J. S. *Evaluation: Promise and Performance.* Washington, D.C.: Urban Institute, 1979.

Yin, R. K. "The Case Study as a Serious Research Strategy." *Knowledge: Creation, Diffusion,*

Utilization, 1981a, *3,* 97–114.

Yin, R. K. "The Case Study Crisis: Some Answers." *Administrative Science Quarterly,* 1981b, *26,* 58–65.

Yin, R. K. "The Case Study as a Tool for Doing Evaluation." *Current Sociology,* 1992, *40* (1), 121–137.

Yin, R. K. *Applications of Case Study Research.* Thousand Oaks, Calif.: Sage, 1993.

Yin, R. K. *Case Study Research: Design and Methods.* (2nd ed.) Thousand Oaks, Calif.: Sage, 1994a.

Yin, R. K. "Evaluation: A Singular Craft." In C. S. Reichardt and S. F. Rallis (eds.), *The Qualitative-Quantitative Debate: New Perspectives.* New Directions for Program Evaluation, no. 61. San Francisco: Jossey-Bass, 1994b.

Yin, R. K. "The Abridged Version of Case Study Research." In L. Bickman and D. Rog (eds.), *Handbook of Applied Social Research Methods.* Thousand Oaks, Calif.: Sage, 1997.

Yin, R. K., and Bickman, L. "Reforms as Non-Experiments: A New Paradigm." In L. Bickman (ed.), *Validity and Social Experimentation: Donald Campbell's Legacy.* Thousand Oaks, Calif.: Sage, forthcoming.

ROBERT K. YIN *is president of COSMOS Corporation, Bethesda, Maryland.*

Twenty years of welfare studies provide a legacy of reliable findings. New reforms will require new research strategies and will risk unintended consequences.

Learning About Welfare Reform: Lessons from State-Based Evaluations

Judith M. Gueron

Over the past twenty years, rigorous evaluations of work-focused welfare reform strategies have produced a large body of reliable information that has played an important role in shaping social policy and program practice. From the start, this research has been unusually real-world in two senses: it was designed to answer questions posed by policymakers and program operators, and it resulted from field tests conducted in actual operating welfare offices throughout the country. Today we face a new world of welfare, where there is likely to be much more variation in state programs, creating at the same time greater opportunity for progress and a heightened risk of unintended consequences. As a result, the need is more acute than ever for hard information on the effects of different approaches to reweaving the safety net.

The purpose of this chapter is to summarize the origin, context, and main themes of many of the major studies conducted during this period and also to look ahead at some of the likely challenges and opportunities for further evaluations. The author was asked to tell the Manpower Demonstration Research Corporation (MDRC) story. Thus, the lens in this chapter is focused on our work, without meaning to imply that this provides a complete picture of what was learned. Beyond that, the reader is cautioned that although she sought to be objective, the author was a direct actor in this work.

Step One: Recognizing the Need

In 1974, the Ford Foundation and six federal agencies established MDRC with the goal of improving public policy for low-income people by identifying and strengthening effective programs. The intent was to provide policymakers and practitioners with reliable evidence on what works and what does not, and to get this evidence via field-testing new ideas in real-world operating environments.

The key to our approach included correctly diagnosing the problem, using a reasonable treatment, having a reliable way to measure success, and having the independence to tell people what we learned. And, because our goal was to affect policy—not to fill libraries—we took an active approach to information dissemination.

Our experience suggests the value of rigorous research coming from a source viewed as objective. In social policy, you operate in an environment rich in opinion and acrimony and short on generally agreed-on facts. You are often challenged to dispel the view that nothing works, that a new program represents good money being thrown after bad. To counter this view, you need rock-solid evidence of a program's effectiveness. When MDRC was created, the problem was not a lack of studies. There were many federally funded demonstrations and initiatives, but they often ended with a conference at which a group of experts argued about what had been learned—not what the findings meant for policy, but what the findings actually were. There was no body of evidence that was widely believed across the political spectrum.

Commenting on this state of affairs, Henry Aaron, in his influential book *Politics and the Professors,* talked about the conservative force created by academic, jargon-filled disputes over arcane techniques. "What is an ordinary member of the tribe [that is, the public] to do," he asked, "when the witch doctors [the scientists and scholars] disagree?" (Aaron, 1978, pp. 158–159).

MDRC was set up with the goal of doing better, and a key part of attaining that goal was pioneering the use of random assignment field experiments to test operating social programs. This approach was undertaken not out of stubbornness or some sort of mystical conviction, but out of a belief that the simplicity and credibility of random assignment would matter in the policy process—that it would reduce the conflict and jargon and sell itself. MDRC's enthusiasm for random assignment also came out of the ethical concern that if you were going to conduct large-scale field studies involving primary data collection, it was important to be sure that the first-order questions would be answered clearly.

Step Two: Testing Social Policies in a Laboratory Environment

MDRC's first project, the National Supported Work Demonstration, was the first instance in which an operating employment program was tested out in multiple sites as a social experiment using random assignment. (Supported Work offered twelve to eighteen months of paid employment to former drug abusers, ex-offenders, long-term welfare recipients, and disadvantaged youth.)

To convince program operators to participate in the study, MDRC staff carefully explained that the whole reason for the experiment was that we did not know whether the program actually would help people—and that, more-over, there were resources to enroll only a small number of those likely to be interested in Supported Work jobs. Ultimately, ten pioneering community-based Supported Work programs joined the demonstration, convinced that valuable knowledge would be gained, and becoming allies of the project in the process. The result was the first definitive study of an employment program and the first convincing evidence that work programs make a positive differ-ence for welfare recipients.

Step Three: Moving out of the Laboratory and into the States

The next critical step came in 1981, when President Reagan came to office with the controversial goal of changing welfare into workfare, in which people would have to work in exchange for their benefits. With many unanswered questions and high political stakes, Congress did *not* enact national workfare, but instead gave states, for the first time, the option to require workfare for Aid to Families with Dependent Children (AFDC) recipients and, at the same time, new flexibility to reshape the Work Incentive (WIN) Program and use welfare funds to pay subsidies to private employers to hire welfare recipients.

The 1981 legislation was passed in a highly charged environment, in which some people in the new administration viewed evaluation as a tool of left-leaning professors. After making some initial plans to assess the imple-mentation of workfare, the federal government decided not to study the states' responses to the legislation. That prompted us at MDRC to conclude that an independent, objective evaluation was critically needed.

To conduct this evaluation, MDRC sought and got a substantial challenge grant (a grant requiring a match from other sources) from the Ford Founda-tion. MDRC used this grant to create the eleven-state Demonstration of State Work/Welfare Initiatives, in which we embedded random assignment studies in operating welfare offices in multiple locations in eight of the states. The idea was to leverage the funds from mainstream sources, creating major new oppor-tunities to learn.

To translate this vision into reality, we met with welfare commissioners in more than thirty states, looking for a combination of innovation, scale, qual-ity administrative data (to track outcomes over time), matching funds, and a willingness to do random assignment. We presented this project to states as an opportunity to answer the questions that they cared about—an argument that carried much weight (see Gueron, 1985, and Gueron and Nathan, 1985.) One reason key state staff agreed to use random assignment was that none of them had the resources or capacity to implement their reform program for *all* peo-ple on welfare throughout the state. In these conditions, we argued that ran-dom assignment was a fair way to ration scarce services.

Administrators also recognized that data on program *outcomes* (such as the number of job placements or welfare departures) would not tell them how much *difference* or *impact* a new program made. Initially, we illustrated this point with data from the control groups in the Supported Work and other random assignment studies. Later, Mary Jo Bane and David Ellwood's influential study of welfare caseload dynamics showed that people moved on and off welfare on their own all the time, further calling into question the "value added" from doing well on typical performance measures without a better understanding of what people would have done unaided (Bane and Ellwood, 1983). Armed with these results, we argued that a random assignment test could provide uniquely convincing evidence of the change brought about by a state's planned initiative. A further argument for this research approach was the clear evidence that it could be implemented as part of the regular welfare intake processes, evidence provided by a number of studies MDRC conducted in several WIN offices during the late 1970s (Goldman, 1981; Wolfhagen, 1983).

Administrators also had their own reasons to join the studies: some were under conflicting pressure from legislatures and advocates and wanted both to test particular approaches on a modest scale and to get objective evidence on which to base their broader decisions; most saw political and substantive advantages in being among a small group of states at the forefront of innovation; and all saw participation in these studies as an opportunity to get higher-quality information than they could pay for on their own. But states also raised concerns: Would the studies place undue burdens on hard-pressed staff? Would they undercut the states' ability to meet ongoing performance requirements? What "treatment" would be offered to people in the control group?

After much negotiation, the result was a series of studies and a new way of learning about state innovations that ultimately inspired a large number of rigorous evaluations of state welfare reforms (Greenberg and Wiseman, 1992; Gueron and Pauly, 1991). Although the Ford Foundation's grant and MDRC's efforts were the catalysts for change, in some sense the real heroes were in state capitals across the country and at the U.S. Department of Health and Human Services (HHS) in Washington. At the state level, I am referring to the welfare commissioners, who opened up their programs to objective scrutiny, and the key staff in state agencies and legislatures who cooperated with the research protocols, provided the data, used the findings, and often became fans of high-quality evaluations. At HHS, the heroes were those much-maligned bureaucrats who, for the past fifteen years, through Republican and Democratic administrations, took seriously the language Congress had put in Section 1115 of the Social Security Act, which allowed states to waive provisions of the AFDC law in order to test out welfare reform ideas, but only if they assessed their innovations.

During 1995, the governors often railed against the waiver process and the need to go to Washington "on bended knee" to request federal approval for changing the AFDC program. Although the process was cumbersome and did limit state flexibility, there is now a strong knowledge base about welfare reform options largely because of the bureaucrats who insisted on rigorous evaluations. The 1996 federal welfare law ends this waiver process at the very time when the replacement of AFDC by block grants to states makes information on the effects of different strategies even more critical; there is no comparable mechanism for ensuring that the nation learns the achievements and drawbacks of the myriad state policies likely to result from the legislation.

The research approach described in this article has been used to test several different welfare reform strategies (see Bloom, 1997, for a summary of these studies). After briefly discussing why work programs have been at the center of welfare reform for thirty years, this article summarizes what is known about the success of these various strategies and then describes the techniques that MDRC has used to bring that knowledge to policymakers. The conclusion presents the lessons I draw from that experience.

The Emphasis on Work

Before it was replaced by block grants, AFDC was the nation's largest cash welfare program. It was created in 1935 explicitly to help a group of poor single mothers (primarily widows) stay *out* of the labor force and stay home to take care of their children. Since then, much has changed. Most important, women have flooded into the labor market (often not by choice), and most mothers on welfare are now unmarried. Providing long-term support seems less equitable and is clearly much less popular than it once was.

The public wanted change, but—and this is where the challenge of reform comes in—it has always wanted change that would satisfy two often conflicting goals: providing a safety net for children and requiring that their parents work.

Starting in the late 1960s, and notably in 1988 with the creation of the JOBS program (WIN's successor) under the Family Support Act, Congress and the states crafted a new basic compromise in an effort to reconcile those goals. The concept seemed simple: welfare should be transformed from a no-strings-attached entitlement (if you were poor, you got money) to a program in which families would continue to get support but parents would have to participate in some work-directed activity (such as looking for a job or participating in training or education) or work for their benefits.

There have been several visions of how to make this mandate real. One vision was work-promoting, welfare-to-work programs. A second vision—a work-for-benefits strategy—focused on the importance of an ongoing quid pro quo, even if it did not directly lead to unsubsidized work. Under this approach, those who were not successful in finding regular jobs would have to work in government-created positions in order to receive continued support. The hope was that participation in work-related activities and work requirements themselves would simultaneously change the values conveyed by the welfare system, make welfare less attractive, and require participation in services that themselves would speed the transition to self-support.

Until 1992, that was the thrust of all major reform proposals, but this changed in the presidential election that year, when candidate Bill Clinton called for a limit on the length of time people could receive work-promoting services, after which their only option for continuing public support would be a community service job. Although President Clinton described a plan that would have required welfare recipients to work after they had received assistance for two years, his language about "ending welfare as we know it"—and the fact that a work-based safety net would probably cost more than just providing cash—started the country down the path toward the new law that allows states to end all cash support.

The 1996 Personal Responsibility and Work Opportunity Reconciliation Act (P.L. 104–193), which substituted Temporary Assistance for Needy Families (TANF) block grants for AFDC, put the United States at a historic crossroads. Under the new system, states receive a fixed amount of federal funds, ending the sixty-year-old federal-state partnership that funded and structured the welfare entitlement. Although there are new restrictions on the use of federal funds, states have gained great flexibility in the use of their own funds, and thus in the overall design of the states' safety nets.

The law is in many ways a statement of faith or hope. Previous efforts to reform welfare have been cautious, incremental, and knowledge-based, as officials balanced their fears of hurting vulnerable people and burdening budgets against their desire to move the system in new directions. In contrast, the legislation signed last year was a radical leap into the unknown. It assumed that changes in government programs would ultimately lead to major shifts in very personal behavior, such as childbearing and marriage. Past research showed that changes in government policy could affect some types of behavior but that the effects were usually modest.

Mandatory Welfare-to-Work Programs

There is an unusually lengthy and reliable record of studies of mandatory welfare-to-work programs. It points to four broad conclusions.

First, there are clear positive results. Many studies show that programs that require people to participate in welfare-to-work activities increase employment, reduce dependency on public assistance, and ultimately save taxpayers money.

Welfare-to-work programs can be fourfold winners: providing money for children, substituting work for welfare, generating eventual budget savings, and making welfare more consistent with public values (Gueron and Pauly, 1991; Riccio, Friedlander, and Freedman, 1994; Friedlander and Burtless, 1995; Freedman and Friedlander, 1995; Gueron, 1996). The most widely cited evidence comes from a study MDRC conducted of California's JOBS program, called Greater Avenues for Independence (GAIN). At its most successful, in Riverside County, GAIN raised employment rates by 10 percentage points, increased five-year earnings by 42 percent, and led to a 15 percent decline in welfare outlays, thereby (over five years) returning taxpayers almost $3 for every $1 spent to run the program. This and other studies show that welfare-to-work programs require an up-front investment, but that the investment can be more than repaid in future budget savings—something very unusual and positive for a social program.

Second, there are also clear limitations. Although changes can be substantial, they are typically more modest: many people remain on welfare, and the programs usually do not make people much better off, because earnings gains are largely offset by welfare reductions.

Although even skeptics have called the Riverside results "dramatic" (Murray, 1994, p. 28) the effects in other parts of California were about half of the effects on Riverside, although the results in the other counties are improving over time (Freedman, Friedlander, Lin, and Schweder, 1996). The findings also reveal another limitation. Mandatory welfare-to-work strategies get more people working, but they do not have much effect on average income or move many families out of poverty. This is partly because of the incentive structure within the AFDC program, in which welfare benefits are cut (often dollar for dollar) when people go to work. When the added expenses of working (child care, transportation, and so on) are considered, people can be worse off employed than on welfare, prompting some to return to the rolls. A final limitation relates to the new context of time-limited welfare. A year or two ago, the Riverside findings looked very good, but now administrators must reckon with the fact that even in this very successful county, 30 percent of the people in the program were still on welfare at the end of five years, the maximum time limit set for federal cash assistance under TANF.

Third, different approaches achieve different results. The most is known about "job clubs"—structured efforts to teach people how to find a job. Job clubs and other job search activities get more people into employment quickly and save taxpayers money, but they do not appear to get people into jobs that offer higher wages than the jobs people would have found on their own, nor do they succeed with the most disadvantaged. Also, the results, though positive, are modest. Typically, these programs raise the percentage of people who find a job by 5 percentage points (for example, from 30 to 35 percent). Vocational skills training costs more, but can lead to better jobs and may make a greater long-term difference in earnings. The problem, however, is that results are not consistent. Some programs—such as the Center for Employment Training (CET) program in San Jose—have been very successful; others have not surpassed the results for a control group. The research record on another approach, adult education (remedial English and math, preparation for the General Educational Development (GED) test, and instruction in English as a second language), is less encouraging. Some programs, such as Riverside, use a mixed strategy: emphasizing getting people into jobs quickly, but also including training or education services. These programs can get the multiple benefits of the different strategies: they can make welfare recipients somewhat better off, save taxpayers money, and change the employment behavior of some of the more disadvantaged recipients. (These findings are discussed in Bloom, 1997; Brown, 1997; Gueron and Pauly, 1991; Riccio, Friedlander, and Freedman,

1994; Freedman and Friedlander, 1995; Friedlander and Burtless, 1995; Zambrowski and Gordon, 1993.)

Fourth, management and resources matter. The extent to which a program succeeds and is cost-effective depends not only on the mix of services but also on the quality of implementation. Spending a lot is not enough to ensure success; spending little is not enough to ensure savings. Managing resources well and focusing on goals are central. A number of studies (Riccio, Friedlander, and Freedman, 1994; Bardach, 1993; Brown, 1997; Riccio and Orenstein, 1996) suggest that many superior programs

- Set high expectations
- Establish demanding standards and enforce the participation requirement
- Maintain a strong employment focus
- Provide supports for work once people get a job
- Involve the private sector in job placement and in the development of training programs
- Target a wide group of people on welfare, not just the more motivated and employable, who are likely to get jobs anyway
- Have good data and management systems

Financial Incentives

A fundamental choice facing welfare reformers is how much money to put into running large-scale welfare-to-work programs of demonstrated effectiveness, and how much to put into making work pay—for example, by changing the extent to which welfare is cut when people go to work or by offering child care, medical care, and other supports for the working poor. More than thirty states have acted to change the economics of work for welfare recipients out of a strongly held conviction that they cannot successfully promote work if families are going to be worse off.

The research record here is much less clear, and the potential costs much higher. Several ongoing studies are looking at the extent to which financial incentives increase job taking, job holding, and income (Miller and others, 1997; Card and Robins, 1996; Social Research and Demonstration Corporation, 1996). A key question is determining which of two possible effects will be the more significant: Will programs that let people combine work and welfare encourage more people to work, or mainly provide more income to those who would have gone to work anyway (and who may, as a result, actually reduce their work effort)? Early results from a study of Minnesota's Family Investment Program show that a combination of mandatory welfare-to-work services and intense promotion of work incentives (allowing people to keep more of their AFDC benefits when they go to work) can produce a dramatic rise in employment and reduction in poverty (over eighteen months, a 27 percent increase in earnings and a 27 percent reduction in poverty), at the cost of a relatively modest (8 percent) increase in welfare outlays for long-term welfare recipients. In contrast, simply informing people of the financial incentive led primarily to the second type of effect: a rise in income as a result of a substantial increase in welfare outlays, for people who would have gone to work anyway (Miller and others, 1997).

Private-Sector Subsidies

During the 1980s, a number of states tested the feasibility and results of getting large numbers of private sector employers to hire welfare recipients by subsidizing wages for a fixed period of time (usually less than six months). The positive finding was that these on-the-job training programs usually got people somewhat better jobs, with longer hours or higher wages, than they would have found on their own (though they also seemed to target more employable recipients, many of whom would have moved off welfare in the absence of the program). The main drawback was that these initiatives rarely reached any substantial scale. Despite considerable effort and subsidies ranging from 25 to 83 percent of wages, only a relatively small number of employers responded, suggesting that employers are more interested in qualified job candidates than in government subsidies (see Bangser, Healy, and Ivry, 1986; Orr and others, 1996; Auspos, Cave, and Long, 1988; Freedman, Bryant, and Cave, 1988).

Community Work Experience Programs

In the pre-time-limit past, even the most successful welfare-to-work programs, incentives, and employer subsidies left many people on the rolls and not working. Public opinion polls have shown that the public favors moving as many people as possible off welfare and into regular jobs and, for those remaining, requiring some kind of community service work as the only way to get continued support. Since 1981, work requirements have usually been structured to require that people work in return for their welfare grants, rather than be paid per hour worked. The research record is thin and mixed (see Brock, Butler, and Long, 1993; Gueron and Pauly, 1991).

On the positive side, studies from the 1980s showed that it is feasible to get people to work for their grants, that they often view short-term work assignments as fair, and that they do real work. Furthermore, under reasonable assumptions, the value to the local community of the work produced usually offsets the cost (approximately $2,000 to $4,000 a year per slot filled, plus the cost of child care). Thus, such programs can provide an alternative way to maintain a safety net for children while sending a pro-work signal to their parents.

On the other hand, repeatedly, officials as diverse as Governor Reagan in California and Mayor Koch of New York City had trouble developing large numbers of work sites and found that some welfare recipients were unable to work, with the result that programs were almost always much smaller than anticipated. Even the currently very large New York City workfare program is small relative to the size of the AFDC and general assistance caseloads.

There is also an uncertain record (and not many studies) on whether mandatory workfare programs actually speed the eventual transition to unsubsidized work. Because of this, it appears that in strictly budgetary terms—that is, ignoring the value of the work performed—sending people a small welfare check is probably cheaper than providing them with a nonmarket way to earn it. This is because free labor is not really free: it costs money to develop, manage, and monitor work sites and to provide child care to people while they are working.

In summary, mandatory work programs meet the public's desire to find a way to link support to work, but past efforts have never reached the scale needed to learn what would happen if support was really work-based. Given the tough work requirements in the new welfare law, it will be critical to determine the feasibility and cost of larger-scale work programs and critical whether states can be more successful in transitioning people from these programs into unsubsidized work.

Time Limits

The findings discussed above all come from studies conducted prior to the introduction of time limits on cash benefits. A number of studies are under way that will examine the extent to which time limits affect behavior. Will there be a dramatic increase in employment, either before the time limit or after people reach it? Will many people be cut off welfare with no work? How will families survive without welfare? Will there be long-term effects on childbearing, family formation, or the well-being of children? Initial findings point to the challenges in implementing such programs: gearing up welfare-to-work programs to maximize pre-time-limit employment; balancing flexibility (to reflect the diversity in the caseload) and firmness (to send a clear message); communicating the message that the time limit is real; and helping recipients manage their use of welfare within time limits (see Bloom, 1997; Bloom and Butler, 1995; Bloom, Kemple, and Rogers-Dillon, 1997).

Lessons on Running Social Experiments

The past studies have been credited with having had an unusually large effect on policy. This was particularly true during the mid-1980s, in the debate in California leading up to the passage of the GAIN legislation and the debate in Congress culminating in the Family Support Act. (See, for example, Baum, 1991; Haskins, 1991; Greenberg and Mandell, 1991; Szanton, 1991; Wiseman, 1991; Wallace and Long, 1987.) Looking back at this series of studies, I draw twelve lessons about running a successful social experiment.

Lesson 1: Make a Correct Diagnosis of the Problem. The life cycle of a major experiment or evaluation is often five or more years. To succeed, the study must be rooted in issues that matter—concerns that will outlive the tenure of an assistant secretary or a state commissioner and will still be of interest when the results are in—and in which there are important unanswered questions.

Lesson 2: Have a Reasonable Treatment. An experiment should test an approach that looks feasible operationally and politically—in which, for example, it is likely that the relevant delivery systems will cooperate, that people will participate enough for the intervention to make a difference, and that the costs will not be so high as to rule out replication.

Lesson 3: Design a Real-World Test. A program should be tested fairly (for example, not during a chaotic start-up period) and, if possible, in multiple sites. It is uniquely powerful to be able to say that similar results emerged in Little Rock, San Diego, and Baltimore. Replicating success in diverse environments is highly convincing to Congress and state officials (Baum, 1991).

Lesson 4: Address the Key Questions That People Care About. In welfare reform, people care about a range of questions: Does the approach work? For whom? Under what conditions? Can it be replicated? How do benefits compare with costs? In addition to getting the hard numbers derived from social experiments, it is important to address some of the qualitative concerns that underlie public attitudes.

Lesson 5: Have a Reliable Way to Find Out Whether the Program Works. This is where the unique strength of having a social experiment comes in. Policymakers flee from technical debates among experts. They do not want to take a stand and find that the evidence has evaporated in the course of obscure debates about methodology. In my view, the key in large-scale projects is to answer a few questions well. Failure is not in learning that something does not work, but to get to the end of a large project and say, "I don't know." The cost of the witch doctors disagreeing is indeed paralysis and, ultimately, threatens to discredit social policy research.

The social experiments of the past twenty years showed that it was possible to produce a database widely accepted by congressional staff, federal agencies, the Congressional Budget Office, the General Accounting Office, state agencies, and state legislatures. When we started these studies, there was a football-field-wide range of uncertainty around the cost, impacts, and feasibility of welfare-to-work programs. Now we have narrowed this field dramatically.

Random assignment alone does not ensure success, however. You need large samples, adequate follow-up, quality data collection, and a way to isolate the control group from the spillover effects of the treatment. Moreover, rigor has its drawbacks. Peter Rossi once formulated several laws about policy research, one of which was the better the study, the smaller the likely net impact (see Baum, 1991). Quality policy research must continually compete with the claims of greater success based on weaker evidence.

Lesson 6: Contextualize the Results. To have an effect on policy, it is usually not enough to carry out a good project and report the lessons. You need to help the audience assess the relative value of the approach tested versus others. To do this, you should lodge the results of the experiment in the broader context of what is known about what works and what does not.

Lesson 7: Simplify. If it takes an advanced degree to understand the lessons, they are unlikely to reach policymakers. One of the beauties of a social experiment is that anyone can understand what you did and what you learned. One strategy we used was to develop a standard way to present results and stick to it. This meant that people learned to read these studies and understand the results.

Lesson 8: Actively Disseminate Your Results. Design the project so that it will have intermediate products, and share results with federal and state officials, congressional staff and Congress, public interest groups, advocates, and the press. At the same time, resist pressure to produce results so early that you risk later having to reverse your conclusions.

Lesson 9: Do Not Confuse Dissemination with Advocacy. The key to long-term successful communication is trust. If you overstate your findings or distort them to fit an agenda, people will know it and reject what you have to say.

Lesson 10: Be Honest About Failures. Although most of the studies have produced positive findings, the results are often mixed, and at times clearly negative. State officials and program administrators share the human fondness for good news. To their credit, however, most have sought to learn from disappointing results, which often prove as valuable as successful ones for shaping policy.

Lesson 11: You Do Not Need Dramatic Results to Have an Effect on Policy. Many people have said that the Family Support Act was based on, and passed on, the strength of research—and it was research about modest changes. Where we have reliable results, they usually suggest that social programs (at least the relatively modest ones usually tested in this country) are not panaceas, but that they can make improvements. One of the lessons I draw from our twenty years of work is that modest changes have often been enough to make a program cost-effective and can also be enough to convince policymakers to act. However, although this was true in the mid-1980s, it was certainly not true in the mid-1990s. In the last round of federal debates, modest improvements were often cast as failures.

Lesson 12: Get Partners and Buy-In from the Beginning. In conceptualizing and launching a project, try to make the major delivery systems, public interest groups, and advocates have a stake in it and own the project and the lessons. If you can do that, you will not have to communicate your results forcefully; others will do it for you.

One reason this research had an effect was the change in the scale, structure, and funding of social experiments that I described at the beginning of this article. The Supported Work and Negative Income Tax experiments of the 1970s were relatively small-scale tests conducted outside the mainstream delivery systems (in laboratory-like or controlled environments) and supported with generous federal funds. This changed dramatically in 1981, with the virtual elimination of federal funds to operate field tests of new initiatives. Every social experiment that we have conducted since then used the regular, mainstream delivery systems to operate the program. There has been very little special funding.

The clear downside of this new mode was a limit on the boldness of what could be tested. You had to build on what could be funded through the normal channels, which may partly explain the modest nature of the program impacts. The upside was the immediate state and local ownership, because you were evaluating real-world state or local initiatives, not projects made in Washington or at a think tank. If you want to randomly assign ten thousand people in welfare offices in a large urban area, state or county employees have to have a reason to cooperate. When you are relying on state welfare and unemployment insurance earnings records to track outcomes, people have to have a reason to give you these data. The reason we offered was that these were *their* studies, addressing *their* questions, and conducted under state contracts. They owned the studies, they were paying some of the freight, and thus they had a commitment to making the research succeed. Their commitment was aided by the fact that such evaluations also could satisfy the Section 1115 research requirements imposed by the U.S. Department of Health and Human Services.

Through this process, we leveraged state welfare reform demonstration ideas into social experiments. We involved the key institutions as partners all along. For the major actors and funding streams, the relevance was clear from the outset. This buy-in was critical. This partnership also had a positive effect on the researchers, forcing us to pay attention to our audience and their questions. In this process, social experiments moved out of the laboratory and into welfare and job training offices. Studies no longer involved a thousand, but tens of thousands of people. You did not have to convince policymakers and program administrators that the findings were relevant; the tests were not the prelude to a large-scale test, but told states directly what the major legislation was delivering (see Greenberg and Mandell, 1991; Blum, 1990). Because of the studies' methodological rigor, the results were widely believed. But the limited funding narrowed the outcomes that could be measured and the boldness of what was tested.

Four years ago, I might have argued that these twelve factors explained why these studies had such a large effect on state and federal policy. But that was clearly not the case in 1996. In contrast to the Family Support Act, TANF is very much a leap into the unknown. Although not necessarily pleasant, it is always useful for researchers to remember that their work is only one ingredient in the policy process, and that politics usually trumps research, when the stakes are high enough. The past thirty years have also shown, however, that legislation has been only a small part of the welfare reform process. It will be important to see how states use their new flexibility, including the extent to which research findings inform their choices and their appetite for continuing to learn from the reform process.

Conclusion

Over the past twenty years, policy researchers have built a solid foundation of high-quality studies of the effectiveness of various welfare reform approaches that is the envy of other fields. In the early 1970s, it was not known whether social experiments could be used to test real-world operating programs. We now know that they can, that the results have been positive and convincing, and that the studies have mattered. But this is no reason for complacency. The combination of block grants and the end of the Section 1115 waiver process puts this approach at risk. States will surely innovate, but having a thousand flowers bloom does not mean that you will learn whether they bloom well. In the new climate, there is less money for research, states can decide not to evaluate important innovations, and policymaking is likely to be much more political. The stakes are high for states because under the new law they will bear the full financial risk of welfare changes. This reality creates pressure to get reliable and objective data (that is, to learn early about any unintended consequences and costs of state reforms), but the politicalization of the welfare debate pushes in the opposite direction. Not-in-my-backyard arguments may be transferred to the world of social policy research: studies are a good thing, but for your neighbors, not for you.

Beyond the political challenges, the magnitude of change and the likelihood that it will affect the full caseload make the random assignment paradigm less feasible and appropriate. Fortunately, states have chosen to complete many of the major random assignment studies launched under the 1990s waivers. This commitment to learning is impressive and important, because these studies will provide critical, early information on alternative approaches to time limits, work incentives, welfare-to-work strategies, broad antipoverty efforts, programs to increase the employment and child support payments of noncustodial fathers of children on AFDC, learnfare, family caps, and other building blocks of state TANF policies. In addition, a number of major studies will monitor what states do under the new legislation and assess the effect of the new policies on families and communities. There are also demonstrations targeted at particularly disadvantaged populations and communities. Finally, although it may prove impossible to use random assignment to assess the total system that replaces AFDC, it will remain possible to use this approach to compare key policy alternatives that will be central to state design choices and program costs. The impressive record of the past—and the early evidence of state interest in continuing to learn—sets a challenge for those of us working in this field to develop research strategies that provide convincing lessons and respond to the new policy framework.

References

Aaron, H. *Politics and the Professors.* Washington, D.C.: Brookings Institute, 1978.

Auspos, P., Cave, G., and Long, D. *Maine: Final Report on the Training Opportunities in the Private Sector Program.* New York: MDRC, 1988.

Bane, M. J., and Ellwood, D. T. *The Dynamics of Dependence: The Routes to Self-Sufficiency.* Cambridge, Mass.: Urban Systems Research and Engineering, Inc., 1983.

Bangser, M., Healy, J., and Ivry, R. *Welfare Grant Diversion: Lessons and Prospects.* New York: MDRC, 1986.

Bardach, E. *Improving the Productivity of JOBS Programs.* Papers for Practitioners. New York: MDRC, 1993.

Baum, E. B. "When the Witch Doctors Agree: The Family Support Act and Social Science Research." *Journal of Policy Analysis and Management,* 1991, *10* (4), 603–615.

Bloom, D. *After AFDC: Welfare-to-Work Choices and Challenges for States.* ReWORKing Welfare: Technical Assistance for States and Localities. New York: MDRC, 1997.

Bloom, D., and Butler, D. *Implementing Time-Limited Welfare: Early Experiences in Three States.* New York: MDRC, 1995.

Bloom, D., Kemple, J. J., and Rogers-Dillon, R. *The Family Transition Program: Implementation and Early Impacts of Florida's Initial Time-Limited Welfare Program.* New York: MDRC, 1997.

Blum, B. B. "Bringing Administrators into the Process." *Public Welfare,* 1990, *3,* 4–12.

Brock, T., Butler, D., and Long, D. *Unpaid Work Experience for Welfare Recipients: Findings and Lessons from MDRC Research.* MDRC Working Paper. New York: MDRC, 1993.

Brown, A. *Work First: How to Implement an Employment-Focused Approach to Welfare Reform.* ReWORKing Welfare: Technical Assistance for States and Localities. New York: MDRC, 1997.

Card, D., and Robins, P. *Do Financial Incentives Encourage Welfare Recipients to Work? Initial 18-Month Findings from the Self-Sufficiency Project.* Ottawa, Ontario: Social Research and Demonstration Corporation, 1996.

Freedman, S., Bryant, J., and Cave, G. *New Jersey: Final Report on the Grant Diversion Project.* New York: MDRC, 1988.

Freedman, S., and Friedlander, D. *The JOBS Evaluation: Early Findings on Program Impacts in Three Sites.* Washington, D.C.: U.S. Department of Health and Human Services, Office of the Assistant Secretary for Planning and Evaluation, 1995.

Freedman, S., Friedlander, D., Lin, W., and Schweder, A. *The GAIN Evaluation: Five-Year Impacts on Employment, Earnings, and AFDC Receipt.* GAIN Evaluation Working Paper 96.1. New York: MDRC, 1996.

Friedlander, D., and Burtless, G. *Five Years After: The Long-Term Effects of Welfare-to-Work Programs.* New York: Russell Sage Foundation, 1995.

Goldman, B. *Impacts of the Immediate Job Search Assistance Experiment: Louisville WIN Research Project.* New York: MDRC, 1981.

Greenberg, D. H., and Mandell, M. B. "Research Utilization in Policymaking: A Tale of Two Series (of Social Experiments)." *Journal of Policy Analysis and Management,* 1991, *10* (4), 633–656.

Greenberg, D., and Wiseman, M. "What Did the OBRA Demonstrations Do?" In C. F. Manski and I. Garfinkel (eds.), *Evaluating Employment and Training Programs.* Cambridge, Mass.: Harvard University Press, 1992.

Gueron, J. M. "The Demonstration of State/Work Welfare Initiatives." In R. F. Boruch and W. Wothke (eds.), *Randomization and Field Experimentation.* New Directions for Program Evaluation, no. 28. San Francisco: Jossey-Bass, 1985.

Gueron, J. M. "A Research Context for Welfare Reform." *Journal of Policy Analysis and Management,* 1996, *15,* 547–561.

Gueron, J. M., and Nathan, R. P. "The MDRC Work/Welfare Project: Objectives, Status, Significance." *Policy Studies Review,* 1985, *4,* 417–432.

Gueron, J. M., and Pauly, E. *From Welfare to Work.* New York: Russell Sage Foundation, 1991.

Haskins, R. "Congress Writes a Law: Research and Welfare Reform." *Journal of Policy Analysis and Management,* 1991, *10* (4), 616–632.

Miller, C., Knox, V., Auspos, P., Hunter-Manns, J., and Orenstein, A. *Making Welfare Work and Work Pay: Implementation and 18-Month Impacts of the Minnesota Family Investment Program.* New York: MDRC, 1997.

Murray, C. "What to Do About Welfare." *Commentary,* 1994, *98* (6), 26–34.

Orr, L. L., Bloom, H. S., Bell, S. H., Doolittle, F., Lin, W., and Cave, G. *Does Training for the Disadvantaged Work? Evidence from the National JTPA Study.* Washington, D.C.: Urban Institute Press, 1996.

Riccio, J., Friedlander, D., and Freedman, S. *GAIN: Benefits, Costs, and Three-Year Impacts of a Welfare-to-Work Program.* New York: MDRC, 1994.

Riccio, J., and Orenstein, A. "Understanding Best Practices for Operating Welfare-to-Work Programs." *Evaluation Review,* 1996, *20* (1), 3–28.

Social Research and Demonstration Corporation. *When Work Pays Better Than Welfare: A Summary of the Self-Sufficiency Project's Implementation, Focus Group, and Initial 18-Month Impact Reports.* Ottawa, Ontario: Social Research and Demonstration Corporation, 1996.

Szanton, P. L. "The Remarkable 'Quango': Knowledge, Politics, and Welfare Reform." *Journal of Policy Analysis and Management,* 1991, *10* (4), 590–602.

Wallace, J., and Long, D. *GAIN: Planning and Early Implementation.* New York: MDRC, 1987.

Wiseman, M. "Research and Policy: An Afterword for the Symposium on the Family Support Act of 1988." *Journal of Policy Analysis and Management,* 1991, *10* (4), 657–666.

Wolfhagen, C. *Job Search Strategies: Lessons from the Louisville WIN Laboratory Project.* New York: MDRC, 1983.

Zambrowski, A., and Gordon, A. *Evaluation of the Minority Female Single Parent Demonstration: Fifth-Year Impacts at CET.* New York: Rockefeller Foundation, 1993.

JUDITH M. GUERON *is president of the Manpower Demonstration Research Corporation, New York City.*

Planning and performance measurement can improve government management of programs, policy decision-making, and the public's confidence in government.

Clarifying Goals, Reporting Results

Joseph S. Wholey

Over the past two decades, budget deficits have risen and public confidence in government has dropped to historically low levels in the United States and in many of the other industrialized democracies. Today we see limited government resources, increasing demand for effective public services, and increasing demand for accountability to the public.

This paper explores current efforts to use planning and performance measurement in meeting these challenges, using lessons learned in several federal agencies to begin testing the theory underlying the Government Performance and Results Act. The paper is intended to encourage evaluators to involve themselves in current agency efforts to define, measure, and improve government performance—and thus to help preserve government and civilization itself in these difficult times.

The Government Performance and Results Act

In the Government Performance and Results Act of 1993 (P.L. 103-62), responding to findings that managers and policymakers are handicapped by inadequate information on performance and inspired by the growing use of performance measurement in other countries and at state and local levels in this country, Congress prescribed planning to identify agency goals and annual

The views and opinions expressed by the author are his own and should not be construed to be the policy or position of the General Accounting Office or the University of Southern California. The author thanks Jonathan Breul, Valerie Caracelli, Herbert Jasper, Gail Mac-Coll, Raymond Olsen, Christopher Wye, Carolyn Yocom, and the editors for their helpful comments on earlier versions of this paper.

reporting of program results (U.S. Congress, 1993). Under the Government Performance and Results Act, planning and performance reporting are intended to

> improve the confidence of the American people in the capability of the federal government by systematically holding federal agencies accountable for achieving program results; . . . improve federal program effectiveness and public accountability by promoting a new focus on results, service quality, and customer satisfaction; . . . help federal managers improve service delivery by requiring that they plan for meeting program objectives and by providing them with information on program results and service quality; . . . improve congressional decisionmaking by providing more objective information on achieving statutory objectives and on the relative effectiveness and efficiency of federal programs and spending; . . . and improve internal management of the federal government. (Government Performance and Results Act, Section 2)

The implicit theory behind the Government Performance and Results Act is that planning and performance measurement will improve management and program effectiveness, improve policy decision making, and improve public confidence in government. Also implicit in the theory are two additional assumptions: that the necessary levels of political, management, and analytical support for planning and performance measurement will materialize; and that managers and policymakers will use performance information if it is made available.

Implementation of the Government Performance and Results Act began with a set of approximately seventy pilot projects in performance planning and reporting in fiscal years 1994–1996. Governmentwide implementation is set for September 1997, when strategic plans and proposed fiscal year 1999 performance plans are due. Performance reports for fiscal year 1999 are due by March 31, 2000.

Planning. Under the Government Performance and Results Act, each agency is required to consult with Congress and other affected or interested parties—and then to chart a course for the future that identifies the agency mission and its long-term strategic goals and objectives (including outcome-related goals and objectives), describes how the goals and objectives are to be achieved, and describes how annual performance goals will relate to the agency's strategic goals and objectives. In their strategic plans, agencies are also asked to identify key external factors that could significantly affect the achievement of their goals and objectives and to describe the program evaluations used in establishing or revising their strategic goals and objectives. (Strategic plans are to cover at least six years, but are to be updated and revised every three years—or more frequently where appropriate.)

With each budget request, agencies are asked to identify annual performance goals, resources required to meet the goals, the performance measures to be used in assessing the relevant outputs and outcomes of agency programs, and the means to be used to verify measured values. Agencies are allowed to revise their annual performance plans to reflect congressional budget actions.

Whether in implementing the Government Performance and Results Act or in other evaluation efforts, we have to clarify what "performance" means before attempting to measure it. "Performance" is not an objective reality out there waiting to be measured and evaluated. "Performance" is socially constructed reality (Berger and Luckmann, 1966). "Performance" exists in people's hearts and minds if it exists anywhere at all.

"Performance" may include resource *inputs;* in particular, dollars and staff time. "Performance" may include *outputs:* products and services delivered to partners, clients, or the public. "Performance" may include *intermediate outcomes* such as client satisfaction, actions taken by other levels of government, or actions by those in the private sector (for example, to control pollution). "Performance" may include *end outcomes* or impacts such as changes in environmental quality or changes in health status. "Performance" may include *unintended outcomes* such as costs incurred by firms or individuals as they respond to environmental programs. "Performance" may include *net impacts:* what difference a program has made.

The Internal Revenue Service, for example, has defined performance in terms of strategic objectives related to *improving compliance with the tax laws, better serving the customer,* and *improving productivity* (Internal Revenue Service, 1996, Attachment 3). The Pension Benefit Guaranty Corporation (PBGC) defines performance in terms of strategic goals related to *protecting pension benefits, limiting future losses incurred by PBGC, achieving appropriate pension protection,* and *raising corporate awareness of the importance of sustaining pension plans* (Gullen, Iskandar, and Tiongson, 1996, pp. 2–3). The Army Audit Agency defines performance in terms of such goals as *client satisfaction, average time to complete engagements, percentage of recommendations implemented, overall cost per labor day,* and *percent of audits with usable dollar savings* (U.S. Army Audit Agency, 1996, pp. 12, 19, and 25).

Opinions will differ as to what are the key dimensions of performance, though under the Government Performance and Results Act the focus is on *outcomes:* results that agencies or programs may influence but do not control. Before attempting to measure performance, agencies are to inform themselves as to the expectations and priorities of Congress and other key stakeholders. To the extent possible, agencies should define "performance" broadly enough to cover the performance dimensions—the inputs, outputs, and results—that are of greatest interest to the agency's key stakeholders: authorizing and appropriations committees, policy officials, managers, those delivering services, clients served, and others affected by or interested in agency or program activities.

The Army Research Laboratory has concluded, for example, that its key stakeholders have three principal areas of interest: the *relevance, productivity,* and *quality* of the laboratory's research and development work (Army Research Laboratory, 1996, p. 6). The Chesapeake Bay Program, an intergovernmental program involving the federal government and four states, defines performance in terms of *administrative actions* by the Environmental Protection Agency or state regulatory agencies, *responses* of the regulated and nonregulated community, *emissions and discharge qualities of pollutants, ambient concentrations of pollutants, uptake/assimilation of pollutants,* and *health effects or ecological effects* (U.S. Environmental Protection Agency, 1996, p. 6, and Attachment A, Exhibit 4).

Performance Measurement and Reporting. *Performance measurement* is the periodic measurement of program performance (inputs, outputs, intermediate outcomes, or end outcomes). Performance measurement may be done annually to improve public accountability and policy decision making—or done more frequently to improve management and program effectiveness. Performance measurement includes comparison of measured performance levels with prior performance and with performance goals: target levels of performance to be achieved in a given fiscal year or in some other time period. (Performance goals should typically be established only after performance indicators have been pilot-tested and baseline data have been collected.) From the perspectives of many policymakers and managers, performance measurement *is* evaluation, though performance measurement does not provide information on the extent to which agency or program activities have caused observed outcomes.

As suggested above, the first step in performance measurement is identification of the performance dimensions and goals in terms of which performance is to be assessed. Once "performance" has been defined, performance can be measured through a variety of means including the use of agency and program records, surveys, and assessments by experts or trained observers.

The National Highway Traffic Safety Administration and the U.S. Public Health Service, for example, use data from state and local records in some of their performance measurement systems and use data from federal and state surveys in other performance measurement systems (see National Highway Traffic Safety Administration, 1996, pp. 8 and 12; and U.S. Public Health Service, 1996, pp. 22–23). The National Science Foundation has tested the use of expert panels for rating program performance (National Science Foundation, 1996b, p. 5); the Foundation plans to use its Committees of Visitors to assess some of the outputs and outcomes of its research programs (National Science Foundation, 1996a, pp. 8–9; National Science Foundation, 1996b, pp. 6–9 and 13–14).

Under the Government Performance and Results Act, within six months after the close of each fiscal year, agencies are to report actual program performance compared with performance goals for that fiscal year, report program results for prior fiscal years, explain why any performance goals for the current fiscal year were not met, and describe actions needed to meet unmet goals or indicate what action is recommended if the performance goal is impractical or infeasible. Performance reports are to include both information from performance measurement systems and the findings of program evaluations completed during the fiscal year.

Testing the Theory Underlying the Government Performance and Results Act

Over the past thirty years, the federal government has experienced a series of widely-heralded reform efforts: introduction of the planning-programming-budgeting system, policy analysis, and program evaluation in the 1960s; zero-base budgeting in the 1970s; management by objectives in the 1970s and again in the 1980s; and total quality management, business process reengineering, and related initiatives in the 1980s and 1990s (see Rivlin, 1971; Pyhrr, 1973; Malek, 1978; Osborne and Gaebler, 1992; Gore, 1993). Each of these federal reform efforts was initiated in the Executive Branch, achieved some success, was supplanted in some quarters by other reform initiatives, and continues to have some influence even to this day. As with other earlier reforms, there has been less agency emphasis on program evaluation in recent years.

Though the Government Performance and Results Act was initiated in Congress, has the force of law behind it, and may therefore have more staying power than earlier reform efforts, every element in the theory underlying the statute suggests important questions:

Will the necessary levels of political, management, and analytical support be there?
Will the agencies be willing and able to define goals (including outcome-related goals), to measure performance in achieving their goals, and to report the results achieved?
Will managers and policymakers use performance information in management and in policy decision making?
Will the purposes of the statute be achieved: improved management? improved program effectiveness? improved policy decision making? improved public confidence in government?

Case studies of agency experience make possible an early test of the theory underlying the Government Performance and Results Act, allowing a preliminary assessment of whether planning and performance measurement are associated with improved management, improved program effectiveness, improved policy decision making, and improved public confidence in government. Unless performance information is used, the current wave of reform also will—and should—subside.

Case Studies of Agency Experience. In 1995, the American Society for Public Administration initiated an effort to document experience with the use of performance measurement at federal, state, and local levels (see Olsen, 1995; Olsen and Epstein, 1997; Newcomer and Wright, 1997). The idea was to generate a set of case studies that would describe agency efforts in performance measurement—and to develop lessons learned that would provide content for needed training and development efforts in other agencies. With the U.S. Office of Management and Budget and the National Academy of Public Administration supporting the initiative at federal level, case studies were prepared by agency managers and staff—and by graduate students, management consultants, and others, all working pro bono. Successive drafts of the federal agency case studies were reviewed by Office of Management and Budget examiners.

The federal case studies explore the context, process, products, use and impact, and costs of agency planning and performance measurement efforts, and identify lessons learned and planned next steps in planning and performance measurement. These case studies are not limited to pilot projects under the Government Performance and Results Act, but instead capture relevant agency experience both in pilot projects and in other significant agency efforts to manage for results. Twenty federal agency case studies have been developed to date; others are being being prepared. Completed case studies are in the public domain and are available through the American Society for Public Administration and the U.S. Office of Personnel Management. Many of the completed case studies are referenced above and below.

Cross-Case Analyses: Preliminary Observations. A team from the National Academy of Public Administration (NAPA) has begun a cross-case analysis of federal agency case studies prepared under the American Society for Public Administration effort: assessing the extent to which key steps in planning and performance measurement have been completed in agencies whose experiences have been documented to date and exploring factors that may influence agency success in planning and performance measurement. This assessment will update findings from the first year of Government Performance and Results Act implementation (National Academy of Public Administration, 1994) and will supplement a report by the General Accounting Office, which identifies and provides case illustrations of practices that can help agencies in implementing the Government Performance and Results Act (U.S. General Accounting Office, 1996).

My preliminary review of twenty federal agency case studies suggests that

1. The most important initial step in performance-based management is getting a reasonable degree of consensus on key results to be achieved and on the chain of inputs, outputs, intermediate outcomes, and end outcomes relevant to production of those key results.

2. Although there had been relatively little consultation with Congress through mid-1996, a wide variety of federal agencies have identified their missions and strategic goals and objectives; for example, the Bureau of Land Management, the Defense Logistics Agency, the National Aeronautics and Space Administration (NASA), and the National Cemetery System (see Avdellas, 1996; Trump, 1996; Ladwig and Steinberg, 1996; and Dolbeare and Donly, 1996).

3. Agencies have defined and measured performance in a fascinating variety of ways. For example, the Army Research Laboratory has demonstrated that research and development agencies can measure performance in at least nine ways, measuring the *quality, relevance,* and *productivity* of research and development efforts using either *peer review, metrics,* or *customer feedback* (Army Research Laboratory, 1996. pp. 6–12). The Energy Information Administration uses performance measurement categories related to *customer satisfaction, employee satisfaction, timeliness, accuracy,* and *productivity* (Department of Energy, 1996, pp. 4–6).

4. Use of performance information was associated with *improved management* in at least nine of eleven agencies and programs that had completed one or more cycles of planning, performance measurement, and reporting: the Army Audit Agency, Army Research Laboratory, Chesapeake Bay Program, Coast Guard, Energy Information Administration, Healthy People program, Inter-American Foundation, National Highway Traffic Safety Administration, and Public Housing Management Assessment Program.

At least five of these nine agencies and programs created *partnerships* intended to achieve improved results: the Chesapeake Bay Program, Coast Guard, Healthy People program, Inter-American Foundation, and National Highway Traffic Safety Administration. In addition, the Office of Child Support Enforcement's strategic planning process helped create a results-focused partnership among central office, regional offices, and states (Office of Child Support Enforcement, 1996, p. 11). At least six of these nine agencies *reallocated resources* in order to improve performance: the Army Audit Agency, Chesapeake Bay Program, Coast Guard, Energy Information Administration, Inter-American Foundation, National Highway Traffic Safety Administration.

5. Use of performance information was associated with *improved program effectiveness* in at least three of eleven agencies and programs that had completed one or more cycles of planning, performance measurement, and reporting: the Coast Guard, Healthy People program, and National Highway Traffic Safety Administration.

6. Use of performance information was associated with *improved policy decision making* in at least six of eleven agencies and programs that had completed one or more cycles of planning, performance measurement, and reporting: the Army Audit Agency, Chesapeake Bay Program, Coast Guard, Healthy People program, Inter-American Foundation, and National Highway Traffic Safety Administration.

7. Use of performance information was associated with *improved confidence in agency capability* in at least four of eleven agencies that had completed one or more cycles of planning, performance measurement, and reporting: the Army Audit Agency, Chesapeake Bay Program, Coast Guard, and Inter-American Foundation.

8. *Political support, senior management support,* and *analytical support* are critical to useful planning and performance measurement.

As noted above, the theory behind the Government Performance and Results Act includes a number of assumptions: (1) the necessary levels of political, management, and analytical support for planning and performance measurement will materialize; (2) managers and policymakers will use performance information if it is made available; and (3) the use of performance information will improve management and program effectiveness, improve policy decision making, and improve public confidence in government. There was little in the case studies to suggest that these assumptions are incorrect. In many cases the picture was incomplete either because the agency had not yet completed a cycle of planning, performance measurement, and reporting or because the case study was silent on some of the issues discussed above.

Review of twenty federal case studies—in particular, eleven cases in which agencies had completed one or more cycles of planning, performance measurement, and reporting—suggests but does not prove that the theory underlying the Government Performance and Results Act may be correct. In many federal agencies and programs, the necessary levels of political, management, and analytical support for planning and performance measurement have developed. In some federal agencies, the use of performance information has been associated with improved management and program effectiveness, improved policy decision making, and improved confidence in agency capability. The jury is still out on the question of whether and when the value of planning and performance measurement—value in terms of improved management, improved performance, improved policy decision making, and increased confidence in agency capability— will outweigh the costs of planning and performance measurement.

Implications for Evaluators

At a minimum, implementation of the Government Performance and Results Act should facilitate program evaluation, which the Act defines as "an assessment, through objective measurement and systematic analysis, of the manner and extent to which federal programs achieve intended objectives" (Government Performance and Results Act, Section 4).

The statute requires agencies to describe the program evaluations used in establishing or revising their strategic goals and objectives, to publish schedules for future program evaluations, and to report the findings of completed evaluations. The required planning and performance measurement can serve as bridges to more sophisticated evaluation by facilitating consensus on goals and performance measures, by providing data on program performance, and by identifying where evaluation should be done to explore what accounts for performance variations.

As noted above, early indications suggest that the theory underlying the Government Performance and Results Act may be correct. Implementation of the Act offers evaluators new opportunities. Evaluators can and do contribute to agency planning and performance measurement efforts (U.S. General Accounting Office, 1997). Evaluators have skills that are needed as agencies work to identify realistic goals, develop appropriate output and outcome measures, evaluate performance, report results, and use performance information to improve management, improve program effectiveness, improve policy decision making, and improve public trust.

Requirements to identify goals and measure performance create demands that evaluators can help meet through training, technical assistance, and technical support. Evaluators can and should help in clarifying stakeholder expectations and priorities, defining performance measures (especially outcome measures) for agency programs, and assessing the feasibility and likely utility of alternative performance measurement systems. The evaluability assessment process—in particular, the use of logic models—can help agencies to meet these challenges (see Scheirer, 1994; and Wholey, 1994). Once quantitative or qualitative performance indicators have been selected, evaluators can help in collecting, analyzing, communicating, and using performance information.

The Government Performance and Results Act offers evaluators a myriad of opportunities to demonstrate their worth in meeting the challenges of improving government management, performance, and credibility. As professionals and as citizens, we cannot let these opportunities pass by.

References

Army Research Laboratory. *Applying the Principles of the Government Performance and Results Act to the Research and Development Function.* Washington, D.C.: American Society for Public Administration, 1996.

Avdellas, N. J.. *Use of Strategic Planning at the Bureau of Land Management.* Washington, D.C.: American Society for Public Administration, 1996.

Berger, P. L., and Luckmann, T. *The Social Construction of Reality.* Garden City, N.Y.: Doubleday, 1966.

Department of Energy. *Use and Development of Performance Measures.* Washington, D.C.: American Society for Public Administration, 1996.

Dolbeare, M. A., and Donly, B. *GPRA Case Study: The Department of Veterans Affairs, National Cemetery System.* Washington, D.C.: American Society for Public Administration, 1996.

Gore, A. *From Red Tape to Results: Creating a Government That Works Better and Costs Less.* New York: Plume/Penguin Books, 1993.

Groszyk, W. *Using Performance Measurement in Government.* Paper presented at the Public Management Service Activity Meeting, Organization for Economic Cooperation and Development, Paris, Nov. 1995.

Gullen, D., Iskandar, A., and Tiongson, E. *The Pension Benefit Guaranty Corporation and Its Early Warning Program.* Washington, D.C.: American Society for Public Administration, 1996.

Inter-American Foundation. *Development and Use of Outcome Information in Government.* Washington, D.C.: American Society for Public Administration, 1996.

Internal Revenue Service. *Case Study on the Strategic Management Process at the IRS.* Washington, D.C.: American Society for Public Administration, 1996.

Ladwig, A. M., and Steinberg, G. A. *Strategic Planning and Strategic Management Within NASA.* Washington, D.C.: American Society for Public Administration, 1996.

Malek, F. V. *Washington's Hidden Tragedy: The Failure to Make Government Work.* New York: Free Press, 1978.

National Academy of Public Administration. *Toward Useful Performance Measurement: Lessons Learned from Initial Pilot Performance Plans Prepared Under the Government Performance and Results Act.* Washington, D.C.: Author, 1994.

National Highway Traffic Safety Administration. *Strategic Planning and Performance Measurement.* Washington, D.C.: American Society for Public Administration, 1996.

National Science Foundation. *Strategic Planning at the National Science Foundation.* Washington, D.C.: American Society for Public Administration, 1996a.

National Science Foundation. *Development and Use of Outcome Information by the National Science Foundation.* Washington, D.C.: American Society for Public Administration, 1996b.

Newcomer, K. E., and Wright, R. T. "Effective Use of Performance Measurement at the Federal Level." *PA Times.* Washington, D.C.: American Society for Public Administration, Jan. 1997.

Office of Child Support Enforcement. *Strategic Planning in the Office of Child Support Enforcement.* Washington, D.C.: American Society for Public Administration, 1996.

Olsen, R. *GAA Status Report and Action Items.* Memorandum to Members of the Government Accomplishment and Accountability Task Force. Washington, D.C.: American Society for Public Administration, Dec. 14, 1995.

Olsen, R. T., and Epstein, J. "Performance Management: So What?" *PA Times.* Washington, D.C.: American Society for Public Administration, Jan. 1997.

Osborne, D., and Gaebler, T. *Reinventing Government.* Reading, Mass.: Addison-Wesley, 1992.

Pyhrr, P. *Zero-Base Budgeting.* New York: Wiley, 1973.

Rivlin, A. M. *Systematic Thinking for Social Action.* Washington, D.C.: The Brookings Institution, 1971.

Scheirer, M. A. (1994). "Designing and Using Process Evaluation." In J. S. Wholey, H. P. Hatry, and K. N. Newcomer (eds.), *Handbook of Practical Program Evaluation.* San Francisco: Jossey-Bass, 1994.

Trump. P. *Strategic Planning in the Defense Logistics Agency (DLA).* Washington, D.C.: American Society for Public Administration, 1996.

U.S. Army Audit Agency. *Applying the Principles of the Government Performance and Results Act and Strategic Planning to the Inspector General/Audit Function.* Washington, D.C.: American Society for Public Administration, 1996.

U.S. Coast Guard. *Using Outcome Information to Redirect Programs: A Case Study of the Coast Guard's Pilot Project Under the Government Performance and Results Act.* Washington, D.C.: American Society for Public Administration, 1996.

U.S. Congress, Senate Committee on Governmental Affairs. *Government Performance and Results Act of 1993,* Report 103–58, 103rd Congress, 1st sess., 1993.

U.S. Department of Housing and Urban Development. *Management Case Study: Public Housing Management Assessment Program.* Washington, D.C.: American Society for Public Administration, 1996.

U.S. Environmental Protection Agency. *Use of Performance Information in the Chesapeake Bay Program.* Washington, D.C.: American Society for Public Administration, 1996.

U.S. General Accounting Office. *Executive Guide: Effectively Implementing the Government Performance and Results Act.* Washington, D.C.: Author, 1996.

U.S. General Accounting Office. *Managing for Results: Analytic Challenges in Measuring Performance.* Washington, D.C.: Author, 1997.

U.S. Public Health Service. *Objective-Setting for Improved Health: The Public Health Service Healthy People Program.* Washington, D.C.: American Society for Public Administration, 1996.

Wholey, J. S. "Assessing the Feasibility and Likely Usefulness of Evaluation." In J. S. Wholey, H. P. Hatry, and K. N. Newcomer (eds.), *Handbook of Practical Program Evaluation.* San Francisco: Jossey-Bass, 1994.

JOSEPH S. WHOLEY *is senior evaluator for Advanced Studies and Evaluation Methodology Group, General Government Division, Government Accounting Office, Washington, D.C.*

INDEX

Aaron, H., 80
Addiction-recovery model, 11–12
Agranoff, R., 72
Aid to Families with Dependent Children (AFDC), 81–83, 84, 87, 92
Allison, G. T., 76
American Evaluation Association, 1, 25, 27, 69
American Society for Public Administration, 99–100
Arizona State University, 45
Army Research Laboratory, 97, 101
Auspos, P., 86, 87
Avdellas, N. J., 100

Babbie, E., 72
Baca, L., 45
Bachman, K. J., 48
Bane, M. J., 82
Bangser, M., 87
Bardach, E., 86
Baron, R. M., 50
Baum, E. B., 88, 89
Bauman, Z., 27–28
Beals, J., 45
Bebchuk, J., 48
Becker, H. S., 72
Bell, S. H., 87
Benbasat, I., 72
Berk, R. A., 59, 61
Bernstein, R. J., 32
Bickman, L., 8, 43, 69, 73
Birckman, J., 43
Bloom, D., 83, 85, 88
Bloom, H. S., 87
Blum, B. B., 91
Bootstrap computation, 67
Bridges, C. L., 44
Brock, T., 87
Brown, A., 85, 86
Bryant, J., 87
Bureau of Land Management, 100
Burtless, G., 84, 86
Butler, D., 87, 88
Bryk, A. S., 63

Campbell, D. T., 32, 71, 72–73
Campbell, F. A., 44

Card, D., 86
Carr, W., 35, 37
Case studies: data collection in, 74; definition of method of, 69–71; design of, 71, 73; versus ethnographic studies, 70; of government agencies, 99–102; historical perspective on, 71–73; logic models in, 74–75; protocols for, 74; quantitative versus qualitative approach to, 70–71; tools for, 74–75; types of, 74
Cash, J. I., 72
Categorical data, advances in analysis of, 65–66
Causal theory, 42–43
Cave, G., 87
Census Bureau, 60
Center for Employment Training (CET), San Jose, 85
Chelimsky, E., 30
Chen, H. T., 8, 42
Chesapeake Bay Program, 97–98, 101
Child and Adolescent Trial for Cardiovascular Health (CATCH), 48–49
Clarke, J., 33
Coast Guard, 101
Cochrane, A., 33
Cohen, D. A., 44
Cole, E., 45
Communications, advances in, 59–60
Computer-assisted telephone interviewing (CATI), 58–59
Computing, advances in, 57–58
Congressional Budget Office, 89
Cook, T. D., 19, 52, 73
Cooper, H., 52
Cordray, D. S., 20, 52
Cormack, C., 50
Critical theory, 25
Cronbach, L., 30

Daniels, S., 50
Data collection: advances in, 58–59; in case studies, 71, 74; experimental designs in, 60–62; multistage sampling in, 66–67
Databases: access to, 59; missing values in, 60
Defense Logistics Agency, 100
Department of Energy, 101

ORDERING INFORMATION

NEW DIRECTIONS FOR EVALUATION is a series of paperback books that presents the latest techniques and procedures for conducting useful evaluation studies of all types of programs. Books in the series are published quarterly in Spring, Summer, Fall, and Winter and are available for purchase by subscription as well as by single copy.

SUBSCRIPTIONS cost $63.00 for individuals (a savings of 28 percent over single-copy prices) and $105.00 for institutions, agencies, and libraries. Please do not send institutional checks for personal subscriptions. Standing orders are accepted. Prices subject to change. (For subscriptions outside of North America, add $7.00 for shipping via surface mail or $25.00 for air mail. Orders *must be prepaid* in U.S. dollars by check drawn on a U.S. bank or charged to VISA, MasterCard, or American Express.)

SINGLE COPIES cost $22.00 plus shipping (see below) when payment accompanies order. California, New Jersey, New York, and Washington, D.C., residents please include appropriate sales tax. Canadian residents add GST and any local taxes. Billed orders will be charged shipping and handling. No billed shipments to post office boxes. (Orders from outside North America *must be prepaid* in U.S. dollars by check drawn on a U.S. bank or charged to VISA, MasterCard, or American Express.)

SHIPPING (SINGLE COPIES ONLY): $30.00 and under, add $5.50; to $50.00, add $6.50; to $75.00, add $7.50; to $100, add $9.00; to $150.00, add $10.00.

DISCOUNTS FOR QUANTITY ORDERS are available. Please write to the address below for information.

ALL ORDERS must include either the name of an individual or an official purchase order number. Please submit your order as follows:
   Subscriptions: specify series and year subscription is to begin
   Single copies: include individual title code (such as PE59)

MAIL ORDERS TO:
   Jossey-Bass Publishers
   350 Sansome Street
   San Francisco, California 94104-1342

PHONE subscription or single-copy orders toll-free at (888) 378-2537 or at (415) 433-1767 (toll call).

FAX orders toll-free to: (800) 605-2665

FOR SUBSCRIPTION SALES OUTSIDE OF THE UNITED STATES, CONTACT
   any international subscription agency or Jossey-Bass directly.